RUSSIA AND AMERICA:

A PHILOSOPHICAL COMPARISON

SOVIETICA

PUBLICATIONS AND MONOGRAPHS

OF THE INSTITUTE OF EAST-EUROPEAN STUDIES AT THE

UNIVERSITY OF FRIBOURG/SWITZERLAND AND

THE CENTER FOR EAST EUROPE, RUSSIA AND ASIA

AT BOSTON COLLEGE AND THE SEMINAR

FOR POLITICAL THEORY AND PHILOSOPHY

AT THE UNIVERSITY OF MUNICH

VOLUME 38

W. J. GAVIN AND T. J. BLAKELEY

RUSSIA AND AMERICA:
A PHILOSOPHICAL COMPARISON

Development and Change of Outlook
from the 19th to the 20th Century

D. REIDEL PUBLISHING COMPANY

DORDRECHT–HOLLAND/BOSTON–U.S.A.

Library of Congress Cataloging in Publication Data

Gavin, William J   1943–
    Russia and America.

    (Sovietica; v. 38)
    Includes bibliographical references and index.
    1. Philosophy, Russian.   2.   Dialectical materialism.
    3. Philosophy, American – 19th century.   4.   Philosophy,
    American – 20th century.   5.   Russia – Civilization.
    6.   United States – Civilization. I. Blakeley, Thomas J.,
    joint author. II. Title. III. Series.
B4231.G35   191   76–43312
ISBN 90–277–0749--9

Published by D. Reidel Publishing Company,
P.O. Box 17, Dordrecht, Holland

Sold and distributed in the U.S.A., Canada, and Mexico
by D. Reidel Publishing Company, Inc.
Lincoln Building, 160 Old Derby Street, Hingham,
Mass. 02043, U.S.A.

Printed in The Netherlands

TABLE OF CONTENTS

PART II : CONTEMPORARY SOVIET REACTIONS

PREFACE

In this year of bicentennial celebration, there will no doubt take place several cultural analyses of the American tradition. This is only as it should be, for without an extensive, broad-based inquiry into where we have come from, we shall surely not foresee where we might go.

Nonetheless, most cultural analyses of the American context suffer from a common fault — the lack of a different context to use for purposes of comparison. True, American values and ideals were partly inherited from the European tradition. But that tradition is in many ways an inadequate mode of comparison. Without going too far afield, let us note two points: first, European culture was the proud inheritor of the Renaissance tradition, and, going back still further, of classical culture; second, the European countries are compact. Their land masses are such that the notion of "frontier" simply would not have arisen in the same way as it did in America.

On the other side of the globe, however, there does exist a country capable of serving as a suitable mirror. We speak, of course, of Russia. That country also came relatively late onto the cultural horizon, and was not privy to the Renaissance tradition. Furthermore, her land mass is such as to be "experimentally infinite" in character — not unlike the American frontier. It is hoped that much can be learned about the present cultural context by comparing the two countries in their youthful stages.

The present book will try to show that Russia and America are indeed similar in their developmental stages. Both countries acknowledge "the importance of the vague". In the following the words "vagueness", "mystery", "ambiguity", "openness", and "contextuality" are used interchangeably to denote an uncertain state of affairs. Most importantly, a sense of vagueness was not necessarily viewed as a fall from perfection. As "vague", the universe is unfinished, and hence incapable of complete rational delimitation. Furthermore, a vague universe, because of its indeterminate character, compels commitment on the part of human beings. As such, it renders life "intense". A vague universe, then, might involve the following traits: a revolt against Cartesianism; a view of the human being as participator; the affirmation of an unfinished context; the interpenetration of thought and action; the importance of history; the assertion of community as providing "grounds of constraint" (see Chapter VI).

In addition, both countries went through a radical change at the turn of the century. This change is symbolized via the Turner thesis in America and the Bolshevik revolution in Russia.

Finally, contemporary expressions of cultural malaise or of dissatisfaction with a particular outlook in both Russia and America reflect (consciously or unconsciously) the importance of vagueness or mystery for any given culture.

Having said as much, it is perhaps apropos to say what the present study is not. It is not a claim that no differences exist between Russia and America either in the nineteenth or the twentieth centuries (or both).* By now, the "convergence theory" has had a considerable number of supporters and detractors, and the argument may be left in more capable hands. The present study asserts merely that there are some similarities (as well as differences) and that these are worth pointing out. Furthermore, most of these similarities are seen in the nineteenth, not the twentieth, century. Contemporary Soviet reaction to nineteenth century figures indicates fear of ambiguous or uncertain contexts, but not willingness to return to them or to highlight their importance. America too has strayed far from acknowledging the importance of mystery. Indeed, the antiseptic world of twentieth-century America seems preoccupied with the opposite qualities of clarity and precision. However, there has arisen in America a series of culture critics who have realized that mystery has been lost and must in some sense be reclaimed.

All attempts to sum up a historical *Zeitgeist* suffer from over-simplification. This is doubly so in comparing two epochs which are declared similar in flavor. The present study makes no claim to be complete or impartial. The thesis here is that philosophy develops within cultural contexts and that a comparison of two giant cultural contexts at the turn of the century is indeed beneficial if we wish to utilize the past to gain a perspective on the future.

I personally am indebted to many of my former teachers, but two in particular stand out in my memory. Dr. Robert Pollock at Fordham University first introduced me to the importance of cultural contexts for philosophy. Dr. John J. McDermott of Queens College of the City University of New York first showed me the importance of an indigenous American "angle of vision", and of one of its foremost representatives, William James.

The manuscript received its final typing, as well as several grammatical corrections, under the expert skills of my secretary, Mrs. Nancy Hennessey. Here again my debt is not a small one.

Lastly, this book is dedicated to my wife, Catherine, who above all people has made me realize that philosophy is a way of life and not merely an academic profession.

Portland, Maine   WILLIAM J. GAVIN
1976

For my part, I would like to thank Janet for her unflagging support and Elizabeth, Damian and Timothy for bearing up under the pressures of final composition.

Boston, Massachusetts   THOMAS J. BLAKELEY
1976

Thanks are herewith extended to the following journals for permission to quote from articles published therein: *Studies in Soviet Thought, Listening,* and *The Russian Review.*

NOTE

* The following are suggested as expositions of the internal historical development of Russian philosophy: V. V. Zenkovsky, *A History of Russian Philosophy*, 2 vols., transl. by G. L. Kline (New York: Columbia University Press, 1953); and Nicholas O. Lossky, *History of Russian Philosophy* (New York: International Universities Press, Inc., 1951). By far the best anthology dealing with the beginnings and development of Russian philosophy is: *Russian Philosophy*, edited by James M. Edie, James P. Scanlan, and Mary-Barbara Zelding, with the collaboration of George L. Kline, 3 vols. (Chicago: Quadrangle Books, 1969).

Suggested expositions of the internal development of American philosophy include the following: John Smith, *The Spirit of American Philosophy* (New York: Oxford University Press, 1966); John Smith, *Themes in American Philosophy: Purpose, Experience, and Community* (New York: Harper Torchbooks, 1970); John J. McDermott, "The American Angle of Vision", Parts I and II, *Cross Currents*, Fall, 1965, and Winter, 1965. Perhaps the best general anthology remains *Classic American Philosophers*, General Editor Max H. Fisch (New York: Appleton-Century-Crofts, Inc., 1951).

Proponents of the theory of twentieth-century convergence include: Pitirim Sorokin, *Russia and the United States* (New York: E. P. Dutton and Company, Inc., 1944); John Kenneth Galbraith, *The New Industrial State* (Boston: Houghton-Mifflin, 1971). A critical stance is taken by Bertram D. Wolfe in his "Russia and the U. S. A.: A Challenge to the Convergence Theory", *The Humanist*, Vol. XXVIII, #5, September/October 1968, pp. 3–8.

PART I

THE CULTURAL BEGINNINGS

CHAPTER I

THE IMPORTANCE OF AMBIGUITY IN RUSSIAN AND AMERICAN CULTURE*

One great problem facing the twentieth century is that of a pervasive cultural myopia. Again and again we define ourselves in exclusive, elitist categories, both on a personal and on a national level. The current situation has reached the critical stage, for as McLuhan has shown, we are now all intimate citizens of a global village.[1] The tragedy of our present situation is that it represents a significant departure from early American culture. Our tradition in general is not susceptible to articulation in an arbitrarily truncated manner. Even a cursory view of such eminent writers as William James and John Dewey will indicate a dissatisfaction with *a priori* deductive systems; instead, philosophical outlooks are constantly subjected to the press of experience. Philosophy in America reflected its frontier beginnings in maintaining that no account of the universe could be deemed complete until the last person in experience had had his say.

In rejecting completed systems and avowing the interpenetration of thought and action the American tradition was indeed "pragmatic". But the pragmatism it avowed must be placed in a wide cultural context. Pragmatism, in other words, is a broad-based response to an unfinished universe – inherently vague or ambiguous. Perhaps the term "mystic pragmatism" would more clearly denote the broad quality of the unfinished context. The mystic tradition is known for its view of the person as being "part and parcel of a wider Self", its belief that God is "everywhere and nowhere", in short, for its assertion that all things interpenetrate. By terming pragmatism "mystic", then, we mean to stress the broad scope of the cultural context to which the individual responded. Although objectivity is rejected in an unfinished universe, subjectivity is not the only other possibility. Previous pragmatic choices will influence a person's present options. Mystical pragmatism then is to be contrasted with moment to moment living and with immediacy-oriented "operational definitions"; it avows instead the interpenetration of thought and action in a full cultural context, as yet unfinished.

* This chapter Copyright © 1972 *Listening*.

Unfortunately, the twentieth century seems to have either forgotten or renounced this sence of the unfinished, ambiguous character of the land and of philosophy; it has turned once again towards the quest for certainty, under its contemporary technological guise. In so doing "mystical pragmatism" has been replaced by narrower, more dogmatic outlooks. Whereas, for example, the pragmatism of James and Dewey allowed as mysterious an entity as God to have pragmatic meaning, pragmatism now often stands for a view which defines truth as "economic profit" or "operationally definable", or worse, "satisfying one's personal whim". While these are tidier views of pragmatism, they are also more dogmatic because they consistently erode the ambiguous context to the stage where it is almost non-existent. The ultimate outcome of this metamorphosis is the announced arrival of a non-contextual situation, or at least, the certainty that such a situation will be reached in the immediate future.

If we look for a moment at the other side of the globe, we find there at least one country whose path of development seems rather akin to ours. Specifically, early Russian culture appears to be both mystical and pragmatic at one and the same time. Furthermore, Russia too has allowed this point of view to degenerate into a nationalistic dogmatism.

The present chapter will outline this sense of "mystical pragmatism" with an eye to reclaiming what has been lost to both traditions. No claim is made to present an objective historical analysis — rather merely a point of view. Recent research in the philosophy of science makes it questionable whether facts, laws and theories can be separated adequately, or at all. It would seem that the same problem lies at the center of historical analysis.

The position taken here is that no philosophy develops outside of a given context. Though any given philosophical outlook may transcend in some way its chronological beginning, nonetheless the context from which it springs remains a necessary, if not a sufficient condition for its complete comprehension. Philosophical outlooks then, are viewed as responses of persons or communities to cultural confrontations or situations. Pre-twentieth-century America and Russia did so respond, and in a roughly similar manner.

THE AMERICAN CONTEXT

The American found himself thrown onto a primitive continent, one where there were no moral absolutes, yet where he could not do anything he wanted at any time he wanted. Indeed, one could characterize the American experience in general as having an ability to live with ambiguity. Or, as the historian Daniel Boorstin has said:

> A great resource of America was vagueness. American uncertainties, products of ignorance and progress, were producers of optimism and energy ... If other nations had been held together by common certainties, Americans were being united by a common vagueness and a common effervescence. [2]

There existed in the new world a continually changing process. One could not afford either the myopia of living solely within the past, or the equally myopic stance of living from moment to moment. We take the religious experience as an initial example.

The Puritans soon became more enchanted with what they found in the American experience than any particular dogma brought with them from Europe. Emerson's entire philosophical outlook revolved about the premise that "every natural fact is a symbol of some spiritual fact." [3] The connection between God and Nature, the sacred and the secular, produced a type of mystical vision that was at the same time practical or pragmatic. No God "out there" would be tolerated. The Puritan errand into the wilderness was seen precisely as man participating as a co-creator in the building or making manifest of God into time. The division of experience into exclusive "natural" and "supernatural" components has never been part of the American heritage. Nor on the other hand has the American religious experience resulted merely in an anthropomorphic outlook which could define God in a scientifically behavioral sentence. Rather is the notion of God in the American outlook to be seen as a radically involved yet ambiguous God. And it is precisely insofar as God can be seen as ambiguous that He is involved (i.e., God's center is everywhere and his circumference is nowhere).

The Puritans were interested in the application of theology to everyday life and especially to society. Their religious pragmatism was "less concerned with perfecting a specific formulation of the truth than with making their society in America embody the truth they already knew. Puritan New England was a noble experiment in applied theology." [4] An experiment has as its prerequisite an ambiguous or uncertain state of affairs. Only in a vague or unfinished situation can the response of an experiment be evoked. In this sense then the whole notion of the "errand" was mysterious, i. e., incapable of complete systematic rationalization. Or, more positively stated, there was an interpenetration of belief, thought, and action in the Puritan tradition. The Puritans were dedicated "not to clarifying doctrine but to building

Zion." [5] God was to be incarnated and man was involved as a co-creator in the process. Since all things were indeed manifestations of divinity God could not be viewed from a distance as an object, but rather the very empirical context one found oneself involved with was holy and had to be responded to. Science and religion were seen as interpenetrating in a sort of mystic pragmatism. The "new world" existed as an opportunity — an invitation, not an object. It could not be ignored and its possibilities could not be systematized. "The opportunities of the New World could not be encompassed by a plan, however selfless or noble, devised by the Old World imagination." [6] Indeed no idea in and of itself was taken as a finished product. All ideas, as James said, are merely hypotheses, vague signs of direction, which must be operationalized or made public before being deemed worthwhile. [7]

To bring this out more clearly, consider as a second example of ambiguity what life on the American frontier might have been like. The following points suggest themselves.

Most importantly a person would have to be willing to learn from experience. [8] His accumulated knowledge would have to be continually corrected as he had new experiences. There would seem to be little use for holding on to a truth that was contradicted or not usable in everyday life. The final court of appeal regarding the truth of an idea, then, must be experience. If an idea is true, then it makes a difference in life. In this sense there was a certain faith in the teaching qualities of experience on the frontier, a certain belief that experience had pedagogical qualities. Experience, in a very real sense, was sacred. Not old truths, not the values of Europe, but the actual experiences one had on the frontier were holy. Emerson once said, "Only so much do I know, as I have lived." [9] In the same vein, John Dewey was later to uphold the need to approach experience with intellectual piety. [10] Since experience was both cumulative and always changing, if knowledge was so closely tied up with experience it too would have to be always changing, always contextual, yet at the same time, always growing. In this sense there would always be an overlapping between thoughts and actions, between what a person knew and what a person did. It was impossible to be either a blue-collar person or white-collar person — one must be both.

If this notion of the relevance of all ideas is accepted, it follows that the whole thrust of the frontier experience is on the future rather than on the past. The past is important, but only insofar as it helps a person to do something, to have better and better experiences. Man cannot ignore the past; to do so would be suicidal. But he must learn to use his past, to create with it. Here the optimistic dimension of the frontier experience becomes obvious.

The frontier appeared as an opportunity, not as a neutral object, not as something a person was uninvolved in, but rather as a challenge, as something to be responded to. Because he lived on the frontier, the pioneer had the possibility of reaching beyond himself, of living an intense life. The underlying assumption of the frontier then is precisely that life should be lived intensely, wholeheartedly. The possibility of failure on the frontier was great, but the possibility of the intense experience was also there, and the frontiersman was often optimistic enough to believe that he himself could tilt the scales in favor of the latter.

FRONTIER AS CREATIVE EDGE

This brings us to the last notion in our brief "thought experiment". Together with the importance of experience and of the future, of process rather than permanence, we should mention the fact that the frontiersman in a very real sense "created" his intense experience. As was said above, the frontier presented itself as an opportunity, as a challenge. But that challenge had to be responded to. In so doing man molded, shaped, created his experiences, much as a sculptor molds his statue out of clay.[11] One thing the frontiersman demonstrated was that any experience had the possibility of being an intense experience, because it could be molded, shaped, created by man.

The word "frontier" then stands in the American context for more than mere physical environment; rather is it to be seen as also encompassing psychological, religious, and philosophical aspects. Frederick Jackson Turner, the famed historian, described it in the following manner:

> ... the frontier is the outer edge of the advancing wave − the meeting point between savagery and civilization ... to the frontier the American intellect owes its striking characteristics. That coarseness and strength combined with acuteness and inquisitiveness; that practical, inventive turn of mind, quick to find expedients; that masterful grasp of material things, lacking in the artistic, but powerful to effect great ends; that restless, nervous energy; that dominant individualism, working for good and for evil, and withal that buoyancy and exuberance which comes with freedom − these are the traits of the frontier. ... America has been another name for opportunity.[12]

Ironically enough, although the above quote indicates the multidimensionality of the frontier, it was Turner himself who announced its demise. While admitting that he "would be a rash prophet who should assert that the expansive character of American life has now entirely ceased," [13] Turner concluded his article with the statement: "And now, four centuries from the discovery of America, at the end of a hundred years of life under the Constitution, the frontier has gone, and with its going has closed the first period of American history." [14]

Even for Turner then the frontier context stood for many different things. It was a meeting ground, a place where interaction took place, a sort of cross-fertilization of experiences. It existed as a temporary boundary of a continually expanding society. It was a stage along life's way rather than a permanent abode, a processive, developing activity rather than a thing. Lastly, and perhaps most importantly, the frontier was a frame of mind, an attitude towards life.

At the very least then the "frontier" is a multidimensional word. It does not simply mean "the West", nor does it simply mean backwardness, or nihilism. Rather does the frontier stand for novelty, for experimentalism, for danger, most of all for the demand that life be lived intensely. The frontier is a journey, rather than the end of the journey; if this notion of frontier is correct, what is important is the actual struggle, not the victory that succeeds it.

In two different ways then the frontier experience is vague or ambiguous. First of all, the type of life it calls for is uncertain. The continuously changing wave of expansion is a context the pioneer was confronted by and involved with. He could not be indifferent to his context; he could not withdraw and contemplate it as a mere physical object. It was, in brief, a "Thou" rather than an "It". The realization that the context as an invitation was unfinished and that man was condemned to add the final touches prompted the realization that all ideas were hypotheses and as such interpenetrant with action. But action as such takes time and time as a reality is irreconcilable with certainty or finished systems. The frontier bent toward the practical could only have taken place insofar as one could live with ambiguity, could participate in a real experiment or a happening.

Secondly, the frontier was ambiguous in its very multidimensionality. It was much more than the physical land or an economic aspect of geography. The entire notion of continual change fostered the ideas of rebirth and regeneration — actually "categories of myth rather than of economic analysis." [15] As opportunity, as idea, as the invitation to participate in the rebirth or incarnation of the Divine, the frontier was beyond any systematic analysis. The frontier was nature but nature in a real sense was holy — once again no separation between the sacred and the profane or the ideal and the empirical was allowed. The price to be paid for the recognition of this multi-dimensionality or richness of experience was the denial of certainty and of any attempt or quest to obtain it. Or more positively stated, the frontier as mysterious or ambiguous allowed the type of mystic pragmatism (already seen in the Puritan experience) to grow. Life is seen as both rich and intense because it is recognized and lauded as mysterious. As vague the frontier compelled commitment and therefore rendered life intense. Also as vague the frontier experience was beyond any reductive systematic formula. In his analysis of American culture in general, John McDermott sums up these points well:

From the Puritans to Dewey, one is offered a series of efforts, alternating in stresses and varying in success, to account for man's most profound difficulties and concerns within the context of ordinary experience. In that tradition, all-embracing systematic truth, whether it be theological, philosophical, or political, was consistently submitted to the broadly based canons of a constantly shifting collective experience. Inevitably these doctrinal stances were broken under the pressure of having to support a more than simply theoretical posture. But there developed a highly sensitive feeling for the riches of experience as a way of reconstructing doctrine rather than as a malleable resource awaiting clarification. The doctrine of an open nature and the perpetual return to the invigoration of frontier language, provide a sense of renewal and local horizon which serves to constantly galvanize energies.[16]

But if the Turner statements, cited above, highlight the importance of the frontier in the collective unconsciousness of America, they also initiate the beginning of the end. By declaring the frontier closed Turner raises the issue of the multidimensionality of the frontier and also opens the way for defining the frontier solely along physical or economic lines. The usual explanation offered for the loss of mystery is that the transition from agriculture to technology destroyed the mythic American garden of Eden. As Henry Nash Smith says:

From the time of Franklin down to the end of the frontier period almost a century and a half later, the West had been a constant reminder of the importance of agriculture in American society. It had nourished an agrarian philosophy and an agrarian myth that purported to set forth the character and destinies of the nation. The philosophy and the myth affirmed an admirable set of values, but they ceased very early to be useful in interpreting American society as a whole because they offered no intellectual apparatus for taking account of the industrial revolution. A system which revolved about a half-mystical conception of nature and held up as an ideal a rudimentary type of agriculture was powerless to confront issues arising from the advance of technology.[17]

While this statement is undoubtedly true, we would propose that it highlights a symptom of the disease rather than the real issue. At the turn of the century, the American tradition seems to have lost the ability to live life as mysterious and vague. That technology had much to do with this is quite true, but the issue itself transcends technology. We would, rather, prefer the hypothesis that the American tradition at its beginning fostered a type of mystic pragmatism. While chronologically the context for this was the American frontier, ultimately the mystic outlook must see beyond local or national horizons if it is to maintain a sense of mystery. This is precisely what the American tradition did not do at the turn of the century. It reduced the frontier to economic analysis, fell victim to national pride, and in short returned to a rather myopic search for certainty and consequently downplayed the whole notion of ambiguity.

In effect, given the American context, an underlying doctrine of an open nature and an anthropomorphic view of historical destiny can generate either a bold, ongoing symbolization of man's humanizing his environment, or a self-deceiving pollyanna version of the world in which the major dimensions of life are lived vicariously.

We would suggest that the relegation of mystic pragmatism to nationalistic dogmatism has obliterated the importance of vagueness in the United States and is in danger of causing the "pollyanna" condition to come about. This would seem to be the very accusation most analysts make of our contemporary culture. Philip Slater, for example, notes that our bewitchment with the immediacy of the present moment obstructs the vague but necessary I-Thou experiences of community;[19] Theodore Roszak blames the current form of scientific technocracy for obliterating our ability to be awestruck by the universe.[20] Instead of fostering a culture which interacts with nature we wish now merely to control and manipulate nature for our own personal whim. Such an attitude requires a fundamental disengagement — a tearing away of ourselves from context and toward the stance of the neutral spectator, "objectively" manipulating objects. Contextual ambiguity has been replaced by the subject-object dichotomy.

THE RUSSIAN CONTEXT

The Russian culture also might be characterized as being able to live with ambiguity. Indeed, the entire history of the Russian people seems to indicate an amazing ability to live with the vague and the mysterious. Though by no means conclusive the following points tend to bolster this opinion.

First of all there is a vagueness about the land itself. Russia is the largest undivided land mass in the world. Geographically, Russia presents herself as a continuous and unlimitable plain; she has undergone an uninterrupted process of colonization, has an "advancing frontier", so to speak. In this context Joseph Wieczynski has noted that

> ... the most important character in Russian history has always been Russia herself. To survey and analyze the historical development of the Russian people is to recognize the great impact time and space exerted upon the Russian nation. Indeed, it is difficult to cite another nation as greatly affected in its growth and development by geographical and geopolitical factors as is modern Russia.[21]

Unseparated by any significant mountain range, its immense spaces foster a sense of wholeness or "maximalism". Religiously, this notion of wholeness gives its Christianity a "radical coloring: It teaches us to fear all 'mediocrity' and moderation, all lukewarmness. Christianity by its very nature is directed to *every* human being; it wants to embrace him completely. . . 'all or nothing'."[22] Here there is tremendous risk — the risk of being involved in making a decision. But decisions can only be made and are only called for in ambiguous and vague situations. The very commitment undertaken by the Russian religious pioneers was seen as intimately connected with the ambiguity of being involved in a mystical wholeness. Berdyaev tells us:

> There is that in the Russian soul which corresponds to the immensity, the vagueness, the infinitude of the Russian land, spiritual geography corresponds with physical. In the Russian soul there is a sort of immensity, a vagueness, a predilection for the infinite, such as is suggested by the great plain of Russia . . . accustomed to facing infinitude, . . . they are unwilling to recognize classification by categories.[23]

Vagueness then, in the Russian religious experience, denotes a type of mystical wholeness. All things are united with each other. The icon, for example, gives voice to the interpenetration of the spiritual and the material in Russia. These are not two separate orders of being. Rather all physical things can be seen as manifestations of the absolute. Icons as such are expressions of God, but not merely rationalistic ones. No mere universal abstractions, they signify the concretization of the divine spirit in time, in history, on earth. From the era of Kiev onwards, there is an intense sense of beauty in Russia, "a passion for seeing spiritual truth in concrete forms." [24] Icons, in a sense, are ambiguous — they signify that matter points beyond itself.

Once the mystical sense of wholeness is seen, certain other points become apparent. No mere categories will serve as adequate representations of the mystical experience. The interest in icons reminds us that throughout the Russian tradition there exists a continual refusal to deal in abstract categories. The epistemological problems initiating in the West with the Cartesian quest for certainty are for the most part absent in the Russian experience. Rationalism is identified with egotism,[25] with detachment or non-involvement. The attempt to arrive at objectivity necessitates the weeding out of the human contribution and ultimately leads to isolationism. The Russian tradition often refused to relegate its mystic experience to clear conceptual terminology and indeed exalted the very mystery of the mystic experience. Zenkovsky says:

> Russian philosophers have tended in the solution of epistemological problems to ... the recognition that cognition is not the primary and defining principle in man. In other words, knowing is recognized as only a part and function of our activity in the world; it is a certain event in the life-process, and thus its meaning, its tasks, and its possibilities are determined by our general relation to the world. [26]

Here we find an approach to experience much akin to the American one — a sort of pragmatism which demands the interpenetration of belief, thought and action. Man finds himself involved with the world context in a manner not susceptible to total rationalization. Tasks, actions, needs as such are not replaceable by the concepts "task", "action" or "need". The mysticism of Russia can be seen as involving both thinking and doing, much as in Emerson's statement "only so much do I know as I have lived." The wanderer or "strannik" is a constant theme in Russian thought: the man on a journey seeking truth, being a witness by his actions. The notion of "yurodstvo" or "being a fool for Christ" [27] designates certain wandering monks, suspected by the official Church, who were willing to risk all "economic" riches to gain the mystic vision. There is in the Russian tradition room for the irrational, for chance, change, for the individual to win or lose. One can gain a quick bird's-eye view of society at any given time by observing how it accommodates the irrational. The nihilist of the 1860's reacts to a society which is too calm in a sense, too unwilling to risk anything. As such the nihilist is on a continuum with the "superfluous man" in Russian literature, the man whose talents are valueless and unintelligible to a monochromatic or non-ambiguous society. The fact that there were superfluous men in Russian literature can be interpreted as a forecast of things to come, i. e., a non-mysterious national-istic outlook which exiled all opposing points of view.

The icon, the interpenetration of believing, thinking, and acting, and the notion of *yurodstvo* — all these depend on the ability to live with vagueness or ambiguity. The icon is multidimensional: it can be seen as merely silver and wood, or as emblematic of the divine. As such it is vague and compels participation. Action takes time — as such it is uncertain. There are no in-stantaneous actions. Once the realization is made that man cannot exist as a rational umpire, the continually changing process of belief, thought, and action demands an efficacious role on the part of the person. The notion of being a fool, of laughing and risking all, can only take place where an option really does exist. Without the vagueness or unfinished quality of the situation, there is no room for commitment.

HISTORY AS MESSIANIC

In the mystic context history can play a vital role. Since the spiritual/physical dichotomy is not honored and God is seen in all things, history is by no means a neutral accumulation of facts. Rather is history to be seen as mes-sianic —as the unfolding of God in time. God comes to be who He is by giving himself to himself in the historical process. Man, for his part, finds himself as a co-creator insofar as he responds to his holy context by building the city of God. Indeed the Russian cathedral might symbolize just this — the building of God into time at a specific spot. In Kiev, for example:

> The cathedrals provided a center of beauty and a source of sanctification for the surrounding region. The word *sobor*, used to describe the gather-ings in which the authority of God was invoked on all communal activities, also became the word for cathedral; and the life of each "gathering" was built around the liturgy: the ritual, communal re-enactment of Christ's saving sacrifice. [28]

The historical dimension of mysticism then is vitally important, it keeps the mysticism dynamic. Man finds himself as part and parcel of a wider self, but he does so only insofar as he too acts in time and in history. Going further,

the only way to respond to the invitation is in a communal manner. Since I
am what I am by reason of what I am not, since I need the context of the
other to respond to, it follows that the only approach to happiness is in and
through others. The notion of *sobornost* is a pervasive one in Russian philosophy. It is

> primarily a theological conception: an organic conception of ecclesiastical
> consciousness which, externally, placed the Russian conciliar or synodal
> system above both the papal absolutism and the Protestant individualism
> of the West, and which, internally, defined the Church not as a center of
> teaching or authority but as a "congregation of lovers in Christ." The
> church is "polyhypostatic"; its members are united "organically" rather
> than "organizationally." The Church is not an authority which can force
> obedience but a free union of believers who love one another. The only
> source of *faith* (the highest and truest kind of knowledge) is the con-
> sciousness of believers *in their collectivity*. No Council or Church pro-
> nouncement has any force unless it is ratified by the community of be-
> lievers. [29]

Again we note the central theme of mystical wholeness in the importance of
sobornost for Russian religious thought. Man cannot survive by reason alone
— attempting to do so leads to isolationism and egocentrism, the worst sins of
all. Only in and through the life experience can man approach truth communally. A richer, more intense role for the person is to be found by realizing
that I am what I am insofar as I respond to others.

Once again we see here in these two instances the ability of the Russian
tradition to live with uncertainty and ambiguity — to herald it in a sense as
the closest approach to the Divine. History is not taken as objective but as
demanding — messianic. History is holy. But to acknowledge the reality of
change, of non-objective history, is to admit the vagueness at the heart of
things. Furthermore, vagueness is creative in that it compels a response — a
communal one. Secondly, the type of "I-Thou" experience found in the
notion of *sobornost* cannot be objectively analyzed. To do so would be to
reduce it to an "I-It" experience. The very essence of the I-Thou experience
consists in the ambiguity of the situation. The other, who exists as an invitation, must be responded to; faith is necessary. But faith, belief, commitment, etc., can take place only in an ambiguous, undetermined situation.
Otherwise the commitment is illusory.

If we look at Russian history we note again and again this ability to dwell
within tentativeness.[30] As far back as 1439, when the rapprochement be-

tween Byzantium and Rome took place and Latinization was accepted, the Russians found themselves confronted by an ambiguous situation. Should they too accept Latinization? Their whole notion of brotherhood demanded unity. They felt, however, that the Western Christian tradition had changed the Biblical deposit for merely "rationalistic" reasons – i. e., to make things neater, clearer, less ambiguous. Their sense of community, furthermore, was completely at odds with any type of dogmatism, something which they considered rampant in the West. Dogmatism from their point of view was intolerable because all were involved with the divine experience, which was mysterious. Again in 1453, when Constantinople fell to the Turks, the Russians were confronted with a critical situation. A great shock-wave permeated Russia, leading to a sense of her own specific and independent national unity. The most famous exposition of the response to an uncertain situation was the assertion that Moscow was the third Rome. The Russians were to build the final city of God, the final manifestation of God in time or history (there would be no fourth Rome according to the prophecy).

Lastly, there took place in 1652 the *raskol* or great schism, a critical response by some of the old believers to Patriarch Nikon's reforms. Seemingly insignificant as an historical event, the *raskol* actually is a turning point in Russian mystic development. At issue was not merely whose interpretation of Russian church books was correct, but rather what precisely the relationship between church and state was. In a mystic experience there can be no sharp division between church and state, or between state and community. When these divide, man "becomes disunited with himself." His vision becomes myopic and he becomes competitive both on a personal and on a communal level. The schism evolved into a conflict of establishment religious-plus-state against the schismatics (*raskolniki*) and peasants (many of the *raskolniki* constituting part of Stenka Razin's rebellion at the same general period). Berdyaev tells us that

> the theme of the Schism was the philosophical interpretation of history and it was linked with the Russian messianic vocation, the theme of the Kingdom. At the root of the Schism there lay the doubt whether the Russian Tsardom, the Third Rome, was in fact a true Orthodox Tsardom.[31]

Here then, quite clearly, a question as to the "really real" Christian experience is raised. God is in hiding, He is ambiguous. Is the Tsar his representative, or is the Tsar really the anti-Christ? This theme and the response to it pervades subsequent Russian thought. The schismatics begin to *dream*, to *wonder* about the future, about change. They do not live in the myopia of the present. They go underground, to the forests, where they organize communes. In the mystical tradition in Russia there had always loomed the dark spectre of the peasant or the serf. If God is in all things, how can slavery be tolerated? The mystical notion of maximalism or wholeness ironically enough contains the seeds of radicalism, of revolution. By pointing out the ambiguity of the situation, by showing the uncertain nature of Christ, the *raskolniki* fostered a great sense of urgency in Russia. The world was unfinished, it was to receive its final touches from the hands of the Christians, engaged in building the city of God. But the city being built by the Tsar and the Patriarch (Nikon) was not that city of God and something must be done about it. Charques says:

> Nikon's triumph . . . was his undoing . . . He . . . precipitated the decline of the church during the next two and one-half centuries. And he had created in Holy Russia a vast body of religious dissent, which was perhaps the real source of the spiritual energies of the Russian people from now onward and which was almost always to be identified with popular movements against authority. [32]

In these three historical instances, then, we can see the ambiguity of the situation. Its unfinished character is laid before our eyes. Precisely as ambiguous, the situations demand commitment and participation. It is in this sense that Zenkovsky is right when he states that Russian philosophy is above all

> occupied with the *theme of man*, his fate and career, the meaning and purpose of history. This is especially evident in the predominance of a *moral* orientation, even in abstract problems. [33]

Insofar as the Russians disdained complete, rationalistic systems, they demonstrated an ability to live with ambiguity and recognized that only insofar as ambiguity — in the sense of open-endedness — was maintained could participation be demanded.

Here indeed we touch on the heart of the issue. The mystic tradition, if it is to be significant, must see God in all things. Chronologically, this may begin in a specific context, i. e., the Russian historical tradition. But, ultimately, if the mystic tradition is to receive a momentum of its own, it must break any nationalistic boundaries. This is what Tolstoy had in mind with his notion of "panmoralism". Insofar as a mystical tradition allows itself to become dominated by characteristics of nationalism, it loses its central element, i. e., mystery or ambiguity.

THE GLOBAL VILLAGE AS AMBIGUOUS

We have traced briefly the import of ambiguity or mystery as a pervasive cultural metaphor in the Russian and the American context. Specifically, the Puritan errand into the wilderness and the frontier experience both seemed to demand a willingness to see the world as unfinished and therefore compelling participation. When William James said it was "the re-instatement of the vague to its proper place in our mental life which I am so anxious to press on the attention,"[34] he was, at one and the same time, summing up the American cultural context and voicing fear that it was being lost.

The Russian experience too could be characterized as vague or mysterious. Specifically, its anti-rationalism, its messianic sense of history, and its notion of *sobornost* seem particularly in tune with the importance of mystery. There developed in both countries a type of "mystic pragmatism", an outlook which refused to separate thought and action, the mental and the emotional, the sacred and the secular. Both traditions seemed to realize that myopia, either in the sense of ornamental knowledge or of action-for-action's sake, was detrimental to man. Both countries refused to absolutize the quest for certainty and its concomitant bifurcation of experience into "subjective" *vs.* "objective" aspects. Finally, around the turn of the century both were faced with a crucial decision − either to expand their respective viewpoints to include man as a global citizen, even though these views had chronologically developed in a nationalistic context; or give up the notion of mystery and erect instead yet another type of nationalistic dogmatism. Both traditions seem to have made the latter decision.

CHAPTER II

CHAADAYEV AND EMERSON –

TWO MYSTICAL PRAGMATISTS*

In the previous chapter the thesis was put forth that the nineteenth century Russian and American philosophical contexts were unfinished, rough-hewn, and still in the making. Both were pioneer cultures in many senses, struggling to build a place for themselves in the wilderness and demanding individual commitment to this task. Both traditions acknowledged and applauded the "ambiguity" and "mystery" of life. There developed in both countries a type of "mystic pragmatism", an outlook which refused to separate thought and action, the intellectual and the emotional, the sacred and the secular. Both traditions realized that myopia, either in the sense of ornamental knowledge or of action-for-action's sake, was detrimental to man. The denial of the bifurcation of experience into "subjective" vs. "objective" aspects was part of a search for wholeness in cultural self-expression.

Ralph Waldo Emerson in America and Peter Yakovlevich Chaadayev in Russia served as harbingers of this new outlook in their respective cultures. They influenced their fellow countrymen to take an original stance on the relationship of man to the cosmos. To be sure, profound differences existed between the two. Nonetheless, their outlooks were strikingly similar in four ways: first, each attacked the present state of his country's culture; second, each attack was also an invitation to rise to the occasion, to do better; third, each placed tremendous value on unity, on a sort of mystical wholeness; and fourth, each left room for the human self to develop within the context of unity.

The following pages will attempt to sort out these similarities, first dealing with Chaadayev and then with Emerson.

PETER CHAADAYEV

Although he had almost nothing published during his lifetime, Peter Chaadayev emerged as the undisputed harbinger of the identity crisis in Russian culture in the nineteenth century. Both friends and enemies credited him with unveiling the need Russia had to construct an angle of vision, a relation-

* This chapter copyright © 1973 *Russian Review*.

ship to the universe. His friend Herzen would later highlight his contribution as that of a "grievous rebuke" to his contemporary setting: "an incarnate veto, a living protest, he gazed upon the whirlwind of faces that spun senselessly past him." [35] The Slavophile Alexis Khomyakov, although Chaadayev's intellectual opponent, nonetheless considered him an extremely valuable thinker. He, too, praised Chaadayev for keeping watch himself and awakening others, at a time when thought seemed buried in a deep and involuntary sleep. [36]

Chaadayev was born in 1794, probably in Nizhni-Novgorod. Orphaned as a child, he was raised by his mother's unmarried sister. When he finished school, he joined the army, fought at the famous battle of Borodino, and retired from service in the early 1820's. He went abroad for health reasons in 1823; returning three years later he was arrested for knowing some of those who took part in the Decembrist revolt of 1825, but was eventually released. From this time until 1831, he wrote a series of "philosophical letters." These were circulated privately until 1836, when the first letter (1829) was published in the journal *Telescope*. The effect was explosive: Chaadayev was officially declared insane, and was forbidden to publish. Nonetheless, he continued writing, and in *The Apology of a Madman* he attempted to explain and modify the views originally expressed in the first philosophical letter. His health continued to fail during the 1840's, and he died during Holy Week in 1856.

It is in the first letter that Chaadayev delivered his most scathing critique of Russia. He saw his country as disunited within itself and standing apart from other countries. Russia, in his opinion, belonged neither to the East nor to the West. The Russian tradition was not rooted in any of the great families of mankind. Furthermore, Russia had no useful past – no past which could be used for the future, only some meaningless relics of antiquity.

> We live only in the most narrow kind of present without a past and without a future in the midst of a shallow calm. And if we stir sometimes, it is neither with hope nor desire for some common good, but with the puerile frivolity of the child who raises himself up and lifts his hands towards the rattle which the nurse shows to him. [37]

Russia, then, had no patrimony, no sense of continuity through history, either internally or externally. Russia was illegitimate. Having no memories beyond yesterday, "we are, in a manner of speaking, strangers to our own selves." [38] This, he thought, was the consequence of having a culture which was based on importation and imitation. Russia was too individualistic; she

had no universal ideas, and was too volatile and incomplete. Chaadayev summed up his indictment in the following words:

> Alone in the world, we have given nothing to the world, taken nothing
> from the world, bestowed not even a single idea upon the fund of human
> ideas, contributed nothing to the progress of the human spirit, and we
> have distorted all progressivity which has come to us. Nothing from the
> first moment of our social existence has emanated from us for man's
> common good; not one useful idea has germinated in the sterile soil of
> our fatherland; we have launched no great truth; we have never bothered
> to conjecture anything ourselves, and we have adopted only deceiving
> appearances and useless luxury from all the things that others have thought
> out.[39]

The above quotes leave no doubt about Chaadayev's position. He saw
unity and history as positive elements; and considered that Russia was outside of history and the universal development of mankind. For him man was
united with his past, advancing toward the future with his fellow men. A
culture could not progress in isolation. History was important not as the
amassing of neutral facts, but as the projection of the past upon the future.
And history was the product not merely of reason but of faith, of thought
and action. A culture destroyed the possibility of its own organic development as a part of history if it divorced reason from faith, thought from
action.

While the first philosophical letter seems negative in tone, it also represents a possible invitation. In *The Apology of a Madman* (1836) Chaadayev
modified his views somewhat, and conceded that he exaggerated the negative
qualities of Russia. He admitted that while it was true that many so-called
patriots had idealized the past, nonetheless Russia had in fact been making
significant progress since the reign of Peter the Great. In Chaadayev's opinion,
Peter understood Russia's potential; he viewed the land as a "blank sheet" of
paper and he wrote upon it.[40] Now Chaadayev saw Russia's great promise in
the very lack of history for which he formerly chastised her. He now asserted
that in his first letter he meant not simply to condemn Russia as a parasite
but to evoke a task for his country, to invite his fellow countrymen to under-
take the project of unifying Russia.[41] If Russians would come to terms with
their peculiar cultural context, they could build upon it and move forward
into history. He thus summed up his invitation:

> There is no possible doubt about it, the world is oppressed by its tradition;

let us not envy the world for the limited circle in which it flounders; it is certain that in the heart of all the nations there is a deep feeling of their life of past accomplishments which dominates their present life, an obstinate memory of days gone by which fills their todays. Let them struggle with their inexorable past. We have never lived under the rule of historical necessities; never did an omnipotent law precipitate us into the abysses which the times dig in front of nations. Today let us not go and deliver ourselves over to these somber fatalities which we never experienced: let us rejoice in the immense advantage of being able to march forward with the awareness of the route which we have to travel, by obeying only the voice of enlightened reason with a deliberate will. Let us realize that for us there exists no absolute necessity, that we are not, thank God, situated on the rapid slope which sweeps the other people towards the destinies of which they are unaware . . . [42]

Chaadayev's indictment had a positive dimension. Russia, precisely because her situation was ambiguous, had an option to accept or to renounce his invitation but she could not remain neutral.

For Chaadayev, the fundamental problem was that of isolation, personally, nationally, cosmically. He saw the supreme ideal as that of unity. Unity for him involved the transmission of truth through an uninterrupted succession of its ministers via the Christian tradition.[43] Russia herself had gone wrong when she had broken with the Christian tradition of the West. The Reformation destroyed the singleness of society. It cast the world into disunity by re-establishing national entities; furthermore, it "isolated men's souls and minds, plunged man again into the solitude of passion, and tried to remove all the mutual understanding and harmony which the Savior brought into the world."[44] Chaadayev carried the idea of unity to its furthest extent. To begin with, it was not simply a logical concept. God was not a mathematician and the world was not merely one among many.[45] The notion of quantity did not exist in nature. Measuring was really limitation, and since God was without limit he was also without measure. It was impossible to tell where God ended and where the world began – this was the wrong way to view the Christian tradition. Chaadayev opted instead for a view of God in all things. To him history was important as the unveiling of God. People who did not realize that history was essential to Christianity simply did not understand Christianity.[46] History revealed what Christianity had done for mankind and what it could do in the future. Once again history, as context, offered an opportunity. No mere parcel of facts, history was the "specification" of God in time.

Chaadayev wanted to participate in bringing about the presence of God. According to Raymond McNally:

> He had an *idée fixe*. It was the realization of the "kingdom of God" on earth, i. e., the eventual integration of philosophy and religion and then of all mankind into one universal Christian social and cultural system. His "kindom of God" was not in the next world but in this one. It did not lie beyond but *in* history.[47]

The unity Chaadayev pleaded for was a project, an ideal which compelled action. It involved a sort of "mystical pragmatism," i. e., the mystical sense of being "part and parcel of a wider self," taken together with the pragmatic sense of "acting in order to know." This type of vision presupposed an important role for the individual, but it also demanded the abrogation of egocentric rationalism.

Chaadayev's views on the self are ambivalent. On the one hand, he seemed at times to deny its freedom and to espouse its subordination to the will of God. On the other hand, his view of Russia's past as constituting an invitation demanded some recognition of personal freedom and efficacy. The true self was free, not in the sense of being uninvolved or in the sense of contemplating its own ego but rather in being free to respond to the invitation of Christ in history. Thus Chaadayev saw a role for the self but not for the isolated ego. One became a self in and through others, not in spite of them.

God had spoken and still spoke to humanity through the medium of one's fellow men. This sense of unity, of involvement with one's fellow men, was essential for Christianity. Man was a social animal; if "we were deprived of contact with other intelligent beings, we would eat grass instead of speculating on our nature."[48] And human nature consisted precisely in having the capacity to receive the infinite.[49] But we could not do this by ourselves, we could not accomplish it through reason alone, and we could not do it without history. Rather we had to see ourselves through an idea or project of unity; we had to strive to realize, to help bring about the presence of God in history; only thus could we be truly Christian.[50]

To be sure, Chaadayev was not a consistent thinker. He contradicted himself at various times. Nonetheless, he was indisputably a herald inviting people to take up a task. Furthermore, his views on unity as a project, involving action and thought, and his renunciation of isolated rational analysis connoted his willingness to accept mystery, contextuality, and ambiguity. Once mystery was seen as more than a second-class experience, the way was open for an active role of the self, through community. To quote Chaadayev himself:

Today there certainly is a religious movement at work deep within men's souls, there are changes in the march of science, the supreme power in this century, and from time to time something solemn and contemplative is noticeable within men's souls. Who knows, these may be the harbingers of some great moral and social phenomena which will lead to a general revolution among intelligent beings, whereby articles of faith which are now simply part of man's promised destiny would become probabilities. . . .[51]

Truly, these words of Chaadayev can be used to describe his own philosophical position.

RALPH WALDO EMERSON

Though often described exclusively as a poet or literary figure, Ralph Waldo Emerson clearly stands forth as a spokesman for a creative, autonomous American culture. He seemed to have his ear to the ground, to be sensitive and responsive to all the dimensions of experience in the frontier context of America. Though he cannot be labeled as any particular type of systematic thinker – indeed, he was against systems – his works served as a catapult, propelling America into an affirmation of the mystery and richness of life, and urging man to assume his role as a creator in and through the divine spirit which is manifested throughout creation.

Emerson's biography is well known, and needs but the briefest summation. Born in Boston in 1803, he attended Harvard College from 1817 to 1821, and after teaching school for a while pursued theological studies at Harvard, being ordained in 1826. He married in 1829 but lost his wife who died of tuberculosis two years later; suffering from weak health himself, Emerson resigned his pastorate, and went to Europe. Upon his return to America he lectured first in Boston, gradually expanding his circuit. He married Lydia Jackson in 1835, and published *Nature* in 1836. Continuing to write at a prolific rate, Emerson published "The American Scholar" in 1837 and "The Divinity School Address" in 1838. *Essays: Second Series* appeared in 1844 and *Representative Men* in 1850. He agonized through the Civil War, supported the Emancipation Proclamation, and continued lecturing. In 1882 he died of pneumonia.

Throughout Emerson's writings we find indictments of the American situation. Specifically, in his opinion, America was living in the past rather than looking towards the future. Her poetry and letters were too dependent on England, were imitative rather than creative;[52] he charged that "hesitation and following are our diseases."[53] " 'What are you doing Zek? ' said Judge

Webster to his eldest boy. 'Nothing.' 'What are you doing, Daniel? ' 'Helping Zek.' A tolerably correct account of most of our activity today."[54]

Americans are too puny, too fickle; the many begrudge the few their success; America lacks a sustained spirit of adventure, and fails to view man as a cosmic citizen. In *Nature* he told us that "the axis of vision is not coincident with the axis of things, and so they appear not transparent but opaque. The reason why the world lacks unity, and lies broken and in heaps, is, because man is disunited with himself."[55] He accused Americans of narrow-mindedness, for instead of viewing all things as interconnected, they cast their glance backward in retrospection. While other generations beheld both God and nature face to face, he complained, his contemporaries looked at God and nature at secondhand. "Why," he asked, "should not we also enjoy an original relation to the universe? Why should not we have a poetry and philosophy of insight and not of tradition, and a religion by revelation to us, and not the history of theirs . . .? Why should we grope among the dry bones of the past . . .? "[56]

In short, Emerson attacked his country because it had not fulfilled the reasonable hope of mankind.[57] America was too tradition-bound and its overdependence on the past was directly responsible both for the lack of unity among Americans and for a lack of creativity on the part of each person.

As in the case of Chaadayev, Emerson's very attack contained an invitation. Emerson himself admitted that his estimate of America sometimes ran very low and sometimes rose to ideal proportions.[58] The situation, in short, was ambiguous and the final outcome was still unclear. So again and again Emerson urged his countrymen to put their shoulder to the wheel, to build a new race, a new religious outlook, a new political state. He felt that America's unfinished aspects contained possibilities, if only man were willing to learn from nature. So far man had failed to notice how nature could serve him if he were able to view things from a broad enough perspective.

The American context then offered cause for optimism; it called forth creative resources on which Americans had not previously drawn. The age offered opportunity precisely because it was ambiguous. It was a period in which the old and the new standing side by side were being compared, when the fear and the hope of the situation called forth the energies of men, when the glory of the past could be compensated by the possibilities of the future.[59] All these dimensions of ambiguity gave Emerson cause for optimism that our day of dependence was drawing to a close. Specifically, the ambiguity of the situation, its unfinished quality, would invite men to unity and would foster a creative view of the person. As he said in *The American Scholar*:

We will walk on our own feet; we will work with our own hands, we will speak our own minds . . . The dread of man and the love of man shall be a wall of defense and a wealth of joy around all. A nation of men will for the first time exist, because each believes himself inspired by the Divine Soul which also inspires all men.[60]

Emerson's call for unity had many aspects. To begin with, he did not conceive of unity merely as a logical system. Consistency was not Emerson's primary goal – indeed, he described a foolish consistency as the "hobgoblin of little minds."[61] Rather his goal was a sense of unity – a realization on the part of man that he was part and parcel of a wider self. Man was a stream whose source was hidden;[62] the important thing was to "unlearn" to the stage where one saw and felt all things as interrelated. This was not something that could be done objectively, for the viewer himself was involved as a partici-pant. Emerson's sense of unity then, was a project, a dream which could be symbolized but not objectified. Preciseness and infallibility were not the most worthy qualities in life, particularly if one wished to "see" the sublime which entered into everything. Indeed, an intuition or a dream might often be more fruitful than indisputable affirmation.[63]

Unity for Emerson was not merely unity of thought, but unity of belief, thought, and action. Precisely because nature was emblematic of spirit, all thought and perception had a devotional aspect. "Things. . . are emblematic," he wrote. "Every natural fact is a symbol of some spiritual fact."[64] Man had to develop, through love and longing, the desire to see nature as a rich metaphor of the spirit. "There seems to be a necessity in spirit to manifest itself in material forms. . . A Fact is the end or last issue of spirit. The visible creation is the terminus or the circumference of the invisible world."[65] The smallest fact then, should not be taken or grasped in isolation, for it points beyond itself toward an interrelated unity. Going further, true wisdom was marked by the ability to see the miraculous in the ordinary;[66] in embracing any common fact one was actually embracing everything, for each particle was really a microcosm of the world. All "facts" were really not facts because they were "mysterious" – they could be taken both as individual entities and as representatives of the cosmos. The world then becomes the specification, the projection of God into the unconscious.[67] God is in all things, so that he cannot be studied as an object but only responded to as a presence.

To Emerson nature was richer than man had realized. Richer in the sense that each fact is more than a fact, it is a symbol; and nature and the projec-tion of Divinity are continually changing, forming new patterns as God continues to reveal himself through the material world. Finally, in studying nature we come to know ourselves, for we realize that we are part of a wider context.[68] He wrote:

> In the woods, we return to reason and faith. . . Standing on the bare ground, — my head bathed by the blithe air, and uplifted into infinite space, — all mean egotism vanishes. I become a transparent eyeball; I am nothing; I see all; the currents of the Universal Being circulate through me; I am part or particle of God.[69]

Though the last quote seems to indicate a lack of efficacy on the part of the self, such a conclusion would not be warranted. It is true that Emerson railed repeatedly against isolated individualism. But he also continually stressed the creative dimension of man and urged his fellow men to change the world if it did not suit them.[70] In *The American Scholar*, he noted that the "preamble of thought, the transition through which it passes from the unconscious to the conscious, is action. Only so much do I know, as I have lived."[71] Emerson required man to see the world with an artist's eye. "The health of the eye seems to demand a horizon. We are never tired, so long as we can see far enough."[72] This provides a clue to Emerson's true meaning. He wanted man to develop a horizon on a cosmic scale and to realize that true individuality and freedom come through others and through nature, not in spite of these. In his journals he wrote, "The secret of virtue is to know that the richer another is, the richer am I."[73] The true individual, for Emerson, had to renounce his self in order to attain his self.[74] Far from giving up freedom, though, this decision actually presupposed personal efficacy. The Emersonian sense of unity was not systematic but experimental; it demanded not acquiescence but affirmation.

Emerson exhorted Americans to a new understanding of themselves and a new creativity. Loren Baritz, in his work *City on a Hill*, sums up Emerson in this way:

> That Emerson's idealism was prepared to find the real and enduring symbol in the commonplace, including the smoke and steam of an expanding economy, allowed him to sing the American hymn to power. His mind was the single most useful mind ever offered to a nation trying to explain the gulf between its ideal and actual self, between its theory and practice, between its history and mission. The ideal was real and the actual false. America was therefore not its past, but its future. The darkness was gone, and man was free to follow his instinct even into the market place,

where he would be a God. Whatever was, might or might not be right, but the eternal future was holy. Despite the record made by American men, the American man could stand erect with pride in the life he would live tomorrow.[75]

Emerson's call to arms was a rich ground for Americans to build on.

CONCLUSION

Both Chaadayev and Emerson are of primary importance as harbingers. Each realized that his nation's cultural context was ambiguous. Both thinkers chastized their country for recalcitrance but also both saw their attack as containing an invitation. The attack could only exist also as an invitation because of the fundamental ambiguity of their contexts. Each thinker tried to goad his countrymen into acknowledging the unfinished character of the situation, which as unfinished compelled commitment and participation.

Unity was an important value for each man — the universe was best viewed as an organic integrated whole. Furthermore, for both Emerson and Chaadayev evil took the form of isolationism. One "errs," either individually or nationally, by taking oneself outside of the "all." To do this is to lose perspective, to cease to be a cosmic citizen. The task of life then seems to be that of realizing that one is part and parcel of a wider self. Though neither thinker can be easily labeled, both offered their respective countries a kind of mystical pragmatism, a view which saw all things as united at the basic level of experience, and asked each person to work towards the "realization" of this unity. In sum, both philosophers argue against the bifurcation of experience into discrete insulated parts; both condemn egoism as fundamentally evil, both see their countries as matrices in and through which the kingdom of God (or the Over Soul) may come to be. These are themes which will be taken up again and again in the nineteenth century.

Certain issues in the outlooks of both philosophers are left unreconciled. Among these are the following:

The question of evil remains unresolved. Is evil merely an illusion, as it would be in the mystical tradition, where all things are holy? If evil is merely an illusion, should much attention be paid to it? If evil is not an illusion, is God as ultimate source somehow limited?

How important is human activity, and hence history? If, as a cosmic citizen, one carries everything around inside oneself, is it really necessary to travel anywhere or to do anything? Freedom in Chaadayev and in Emerson often seems closely aligned to evil. One is free *from* the whole; but if one is free only in terms of separation, is one free *to* do anything?

Lastly, the relation of religion to politics is left unreconciled in Emerson and Chaadayev. For example, if, as in the mystic tradition, God is in all things, then pro-slavery laws are basically irreligious. Emerson glimpsed this ramification of his supposed "transcendentalism" and hence agonized about slavery. However, he never seems to have successfully reconciled politics and religion. Later, the inability to construct this marriage will result in science being substituted for religion, and the attempt to reconcile politics and science.

CHAPTER III

HERZEN AND JAMES:
FREEDOM AS RADICAL

Freedom is often reduced to a theoretical problem, instead of being responded to in its radical form — as a hypothesis, the proof of which is in the acting. Two philosophers who continually strove to keep the radical edge of freedom sharpened were Alexander Herzen and William James. Although differing in many respects, nonetheless on this specific issue they had much in common.

ALEXANDER HERZEN

Alexander Herzen, born in Moscow in 1812, graduated from the University of Moscow in 1834. Several events, beginning even in his early life, indicate his preoccupation with freedom. Lossky tells us that Herzen was at the coronation of Nicolas after the execution of the Decembrists, and that, then thirteen years of age, he vowed to avenge the victims, to devote himself to the struggle against the throne and what it stood for.[66] At the university Herzen became involved in a political-philosophical circle, was subsequently imprisoned and exiled for five years. Upon returning to Moscow, he again spoke out unguardedly and was exiled, this time to Novgorod. Zenkovsky notes several events in the 1840's which tended to increase Herzen's sense of freedom.[77] In 1842, for example, his friend Passek died, and Herzen wrote that death was "a mystery — a menacing and frightful mystery." Herzen's own child died in the same year and he wrote, "How outrageous is the power of chance;" and again, in 1844 when his eldest son was taken suddenly ill, he noted, "What a frightful *slough of chances* envelops man's life."

In 1846 Herzen inherited a large sum of money, and shortly thereafter emigrated to Europe. He had great hopes for the 1848 Revolution, but these were disappointed — an event which caused him to realize the uncertainty of history. He remained in Europe for the rest of his life, communicating with various Russian *émigrés*, organized the journal *Kolokol* (The Bell) in 1852 and finally died in Paris in 1870.

Herzen could not "prove" freedom, like one might prove that 2 and 2 are 4, but he could prove it by example. His life is a "bearing witness," a giving evidence to the thesis that one is free. Indeed, he would have it no other way:

to prove freedom logically would be to reduce it to a problem rather than affirming it as an activity. Note for example the emphasis in this late text (1868):

> Throughout the ages man has sought to find his autonomy, his freedom, and influenced by necessity, does not want to do anything other than what he desires; he does not want to be either a passive grave-digger of the past, nor an unconscious midwife of the future; history for him is his free and essential work. He believes in his freedom no less than he believes in the existence of the external world as it appears to him because he believes his eyes and because without this faith he could not take a single step. Moral freedom is, thus, a psychological reality or, if you like, an anthropological reality.[78]

Here the attempt is made to take freedom at face value; it is not a problem to be solved; it can neither be proven nor disproven. Part of Herzen's "proof" of freedom is man's need to believe it. The issue of freedom itself compels a decision to be made — "before all the evidence is in." Furthermore, we cannot get outside the issue and analyze it like an umpire. "Physiology flings the idol [of free will] off its pedestal and completely denies freedom. Yet the idea of freedom has still to be analyzed as a phenomenal need of the human mind, as a psychological reality."[79]

Freedom then cannot be decided in an impartial manner. Herzen's plea is to man's need. Going further, the "proof of the pudding is in the eating", with respect to freedom. The belief I have is that I am free, and, since belief is a tendency towards action, the belief I hold in and of itself, if acted on, constitutes a kind of proof of freedom. Freedom is "proven" by being born to witness via action.

If the notion of freedom is once understood in its radicalness, other aspects of Herzen's outlook fall into place. He might be viewed as having performed a "thought experiment," of asking himself "What kind of a universe would there be if man were free? " His answer might include the following: (a) An unfinished processive universe, tinged with uncertainty; (b) The interpenetration of thinking and doing, giving rise to an efficacious sense of the person.

THE CONTEXT: AN UNFINISHED, UNCERTAIN UNIVERSE

Freedom, for Herzen, was the response of an individual to a context. He believed that man was free, not in spite of everything and everyone else, but in and through the matrix of experience. Man's path has not been predetermined. "Nature has hinted only vaguely, in the most general terms, at her intentions, and has left all the details to the will of man, circumstances, climate, and a thousand conflicts."[80] A person then is "at home" in both nature and history, but in neither of these is man the absolute master. Freedom, precisely because it is a process, is intimately bound up with context, with responding to the invitation of a situation. Man was free then, not only in terms of having been let loose from some overarching sense of predestination, but also in the sense of having possibilities of living in a "space of options," of being free to accomplish something through individual effort. "Man is freer than is usually believed. He depends a great deal on his environment, but not as much as he surrenders to it. A large part of our destiny lies in our hands. One should grasp it and not let it go."[81] Man's freedom then, was not atomistic, but rather consisted in the process of responding to the press of experience. For this view to make sense, the universe had to be posited as continuously changing and uncertain. "When there is danger there is hope!"[82]

Herzen consistently rejected the attempt to label the universe in a fixed, finished manner. In his autobiography for example, he refers to his aversion for people who, either through stupidity or laziness, "never get beyond a mere label, who are brought up short by a single bad action or a false position, either chastely shutting their eyes to it or pushing it roughly from them."[83] Looking at people as complex, self-developing entities compelled rejection of neat answers, of formulas or appeals to a finite set of supposedly neutral facts. "Facts are only a collection of uniform material, and not a living growth, however complete the sum of the various parts."[84] The overly naturalist approach to experience, in Herzen's opinion, emphasized far too much the "passivity" of the human person. "There is a tendency to perceive the mind as a passive receptacle, a kind of mirror which would reflect the given without modifying it, ... mechanically,"[85] automatically. While the alternative of idealism offered man a higher role in the process, it did so (as Herzen was later to realize) at too high a price – identifying the real and the rational. In brief, both empiricism and idealism were inadequate, and each in its own way was seeking certainty.

A second type of certainty condemned by Herzen was formalism, for an *a priori* approach to experience would also entail the giving up of the ambiguity and uncertainty of the unfinished context. As early as his "idealistic" period (early 1840's), Herzen argued against the Right Wing Hegelians for being too content with the many speculative systems of thought. In his opinion, the Russian temperament did not lend itself to exclusive preoccupation with theory.[86] And we can see why immediately — this would have turned freedom back into a mere theoretical problem, which for Herzen it most emphatically was not. Freedom, taken in its radicalness, compelled the acceptance of chance in the universe. Intellectual sobriety, i. e., thought for thought's sake, can be a dangerous thing, in that it often lulls the human person to sleep. "Audacity is on some occasions superior to profound wisdom."[87] A story in Herzen's memoirs catches the issue well:

> Nothing is easier than to sit like Father Matthew, in the seat of judgment and condemn drunkness, while you are yourself intoxicated with sobriety; nothing simpler than to sit at your own tea-table and marvel at servants, because they *will* go to the teashop instead of drinking their tea at home, where it would cost them less.[88]

Although it might clearly be the more "reasonable" approach to save money and stay at home, life, in Herzen's opinion, was not all that cut and dry. Within his later outlook the universe was seen as ambiguous. Life, in short, is more subtle than any given formula.

A third and final type of certainty renounced by Herzen was the uncritical acceptance of the past. One could use the past to get a clearer view of the present, and hence into the future,[89] i. e., one could adopt a processive viewpoint. But when the "present rests exclusively on the past, it is inadequately supported."[90] Herzen condemned hiding in the past, to the extent that no idea would presently be seen as a hypothesis. Uncritical acceptance of tradition entailed a direct denial of the possibility that the future could be different from the past, and hence also a denial of freedom and possibility. It is in this sense that we might best understand Herzen's text: "The Terror executed men but our task is easier; we are called upon to execute institutions, destroy beliefs, break prejudices, shatter hopes of any return to the past, holding nothing sacred, making no concessions, showing no mercy."[91]

The past *qua* past must be renounced; but the past as part of the temporal process is essential. Without it one would be living from moment to moment, and hence never growing in self-realization.

THINKING AND DOING: THE EFFICACY OF THE HUMAN PERSON

True freedom for Herzen involves the interpenetration of thinking and doing. Thinking without doing is no longer sufficient. In prior ages, for example, "much was forgiven for love of science. But that time has passed.

Platonic love is no longer sufficient: we are realists and desire love translated into action."[92] Thought without action then was vacuous because it was too self-enclosed. Only insofar as one implemented thought, now viewed as hypothesis, by acting it out in the unfinished context, did one take on true freedom. Thought then was essentially uncertain because it was unfinished. Thinking, in short, involved both believing and doing.

> Only that becomes our very own which has been acquired by labour and suffering; that which comes by the windfall is of little value to us. The gambler flings his gold away by the handful. What would have been the point of testing Abraham if the sacrifice of Isaac had meant nothing to him? [93]

Two points seem obvious in this text. First, as we have seen, all thinking must be translated into action. Secondly, action without thought, or merely fortuitous action, is also of little value. Action for action's sake is as misleading as thinking without action. Herzen is here articulating a view of the human person that is neither simply cognitive nor simply practical. In his later work, he rejects the view that the person is defined by historical events or by society. He did not believe that any end, or final cause or universal idea was sufficient justification for the sacrifice of the human individual. Also the person was not to be seen as a ready-made substance. Herzen views man as going through the process of self-realization via the continual interpenetration of thinking and doing. Only so much do I know as I have done; and doing without knowing is fruitless. "It is only in the intelligent, morally free and vehemently energetic action that man arrives at the actuality of his personality."[94] The phenomenon of freedom, in short, viewed as a process, has both a cognitive and a practical aspect.

A danger immediately confronting one who gives up certainty and objectivity, as Herzen did, is how not to lapse into simple subjectivity. Herzen tried (with limited success) to avoid this in two ways: by positing a developmental organic self and by positing a self-realization process in and through the peasant community. His view of the self was a processive one — man was an organism who came into being via interaction with environment.

> Separate an organ from the organism and it will cease to be the conductor of life and become a dead thing, while the organism, in its turn deprived of the organs, will become a mutilated corpse, a conglomerate of particles. Life is unity persisting in variety, the unity of the whole and the parts; when the bond between them is sundered and the unity which serves to

bind and protect is broken, each point starts on its own process and the death and decay of the corpse ensues with the complete liberation of the parts.[95]

Life then was to be seen as a process, not a series of moment to moment episodes. The efficacy of the self was to be preserved through the process of self-realization. Freedom to do anything one wanted at any time one wanted would be acontextual, i. e., it would be a new form of certainty.

Secondly, the individual was free in and through the matrix of human brotherhood. I can become a fuller, more developed self by interacting with the community. "The real point is not to fulminate against egoism and extol brotherhood, for the one will never overcome the other, but to reunite freely and harmoniously these two ineradicable elements of human life"[96] Since thinking requires doing, and doing takes place in a context, the situation or context is itself important; it gives one the "opportunity" to be free. Furthermore the more varied or multidimensional the context, the greater the possibilities of freedom. A communal context is better than an individual one because of the very ambiguity multidimensionality carries. The community, however, must remain decentralized to maintain its ambiguity. Herzen liked the Russian peasant commune with its strong aversion to every form of private landed property.[97] He saw the future of Russia as lying with the "moujik," and noted that the prototype of the commune was the family[98] owning all things in common. To be sure, Herzen did not develop sufficiently his views on the peasant commune. But one can at least see there his attempt to highlight the importance of intersubjectivity, in terms of the importance of the context. True freedom demands the recognition of a processive context. "The awareness of independence does not necessarily imply a break with the milieu. Self-reliance does not necessarily involve hostility to society."[99]

Herzen may be viewed in many ways. To be sure, his philosophy is not completely systematic. But one way of looking at him is via the notion of freedom. Herzen realized that freedom vs. determinism was not a theoretical problem which could be solved, but rather an issue which had to be decided before all the evidence was in. From this, several things followed. First, the interpenetration of emotions, thoughts, and actions was asserted. Part of the proof of freedom was man's need to believe it. Also, freedom, since it couldn't be proved, was a hypothesis which had to be acted on. This required the positing of a context through which action might take place. The context Herzen proposed was essentially unfinished, still in process. Also the context included not only nature, but society too, considered as community. To be sure, Herzen was sketchy in these thoughts. Also, there are passages in his works where he seems quite pessimistic regarding the ability of society to function as context. Oftentimes he seems to see individual growth taking place *in spite of* society.[100] So too he often rejects the past entirely, instead of viewing it as useful for advancement into the future. Nonetheless, his work at some points highlights the realization that freedom means ambiguity, that only in an ambiguous universe can radical freedom be posited, and that only in an ambiguous context is a truly efficacious role given to the human person, in and through the matrix of community.

WILLIAM JAMES

William James was born in New York City in 1842. By the time he was 21, he had been to Europe five times. He received an M. D. from Harvard in 1869, and began to teach there in 1873. He wrote at a steady pace, producing *The Principles of Psychology* in 1890, *The Will to Believe* in 1897, *The Varieties of Religious Experience* in 1901 and *Pragmatism* in 1906. He died at his home in Chocorua, New Hampshire, in 1910.

James himself was never physically well and went through a period of severe depression and recovery during 1869—70. By focusing on this period we may receive a hint of how radical a view of freedom he espoused.

On 1st February 1870 he notes in his diary: "Today I about touched bottom, and perceive plainly that I must face the choice with open eyes: shall I frankly throw the moral business overboard, as one unsuited to my innate aptitudes, or shall I follow it, and it alone, making everything else merely stuff for it? "[101]

Between February and April of that year James read Renouvier's *Essays* and underwent a remarkable change. We find in his diary:

I think that yesterday was a crisis in my life. I finished the first part of Renouvier's second "Essais" and see no reason why his definition of Free Will — "The sustaining of a thought *because I choose to* when I might have other thoughts" — need be the definition of an illusion. At any rate, I will assume for the present — until next year — that it is no illusion. My first act of free will shall be to believe in free will . . . Not in maxims, not in *Anschauungen*, but in accumulated *acts* of thought lies salvation . . . Life shall [be built in] doing and suffering and creating.[102]

Note here that James realized that freedom could not be "proved" like a theorem. One could argue persuasively for it, but ultimately, the proof of the pudding was in the eating. Freedom at its most radical was a hypothesis; the issue was not a purely intellectual one. A person's needs were involved, as well as his intelligence. James was later to formulate the issue as follows:

> *Our passional nature not only lawfully may, but must decide an option between propositions, whenever it is a genuine option that cannot by its nature be decided on intellectual grounds; for to say, under such circumstances, "Do not decide, but leave the question open" is, itself, a passional decision – just like deciding yes or no, – and is attended with the same risk of losing the truth.*[103]

Freedom at its most radical transcended the boundary of being a logical concept and compelled action. In attempting to maintain this sense of freedom, James posited an unfinished universe and gave the human person an efficacious role.

THE EFFICACY OF THE HUMAN PERSON IN THE "STREAM OF CONSCIOUSNESS"

As early as *The Principles of Psychology*, James was building the power of the self into the mainstream of his thought. He developed a fivefold notion of consciousness.[104] First, there are no impersonal conscious thoughts existing as transcendental spectators. Every thought is "owned." Secondly, every act of consciousness is purposive: it "intends" or is constitutive of an object of consciousness. There is no such thing as a thought which is not "of an object." All consciousness is bipolar or intentional. Thirdly, and most importantly, consciousness is always choosing, creating a foreground-background experience, whether on the perceptual or conceptual level. We select certain sounds to hear, certain colors to see; we select one perspectival view of the table as the really real one; we adopt one conceptual framework over another. "Out of what is in itself an undistinguishable, swarming *continuum*, devoid of distinction or emphasis, our senses make for us, by attending to this motion and ignoring that, a world full of contrasts, of sharp accents, of abrupt changes, of picturesque light and shade."[105]

But this is only half the story. Consciousness is condemned to be selective precisely because it is continuously changing. We never have the same thought twice, yet we never have an entirely new thought. At the very least the time of any two ideas is different. "Experience is remoulding us at every moment, and our mental reaction on every given thing is really a resultant of our experience of the whole world up to that date."[106] On the other hand, consciousness has both substantive and relational aspects, such that there is a sense of continuity running throughout our thoughts. "Into the awareness of the thunder itself the awareness of the previous silence creeps and continues; for what we hear when the thunder crashes is not thunder *pure*, but thunder-breaking-upon-silence-and-contrasting-with-it."[107] Consciousness then is a continuously changing stream with a shifting focus. In each conscious experience, there is always a main substantive aspect, arrived at in accordance with our needs at the time, and surrounded by a periphery of transitional fringes, i. e., that this point chosen as substantive is *not* that, is *part* of this larger whole, is *like* that in one respect but not in another, etc. Putting the continuous and the changing aspects of consciousness together we get a view of every image in consciousness as "steeped and dyed in the free water that flows round it. With it goes the sense of its relations, near and remote, the dying echo of whence it came to us, the dawning sense of whither it is to lead."[108] For example, if one were to recite "a, b, c, d, e, f, g", at the moment when you focus on "d" neither "a, b, c" nor "e, f, g" is out of your consciousness altogether, but are available on the fringe.[109]

Both the empiricist and the rationalist traditions were at fault here; both refused to recognize the reality of the transitive aspects of consciousness. On the one hand, "sensationalists," like Hume, have been unable to find "named" relational feelings in consciousness; they have therefore denied the existence of these relations both inside consciousness and outside in the world.[110]

The "intellectualists," however, have fared no better; they too have been unable to find distinct relational feelings in consciousness but they have drawn the opposite conclusion. The transitional relations

are known ... by something that lies on an entirely different plane, by an *actus purus* of Thought, Intellect, or Reason, all written with capitals and considered to mean something unutterably superior to any fact of sensibility whatever.[111]

James viewed both of these positions as inadequate because they systematically refused to recognize large parts of the stream of consciousness.

Note carefully what James has done here. Consciousness is at all times a selecting agency. But to select is to "select from," i. e., it demands an ambiguous indeterminate context. Selecting is an activity performed by focusing on a particular point and relegating other aspects to the fringe. James' continuously changing stream of consciousness is what allows selectivity to go on.

On the other hand, selection is a cumulative process, it is unfinished and therefore leads to a continuously changing stream. There is *more* to consciousness than we have realized; it has transitive parts as well as substantive ones, and it has a temporal aspect. The richness of consciousness forces us to focus, i. e., to exercise freedom.

Perhaps the best sentence in this regard, in *The Principles*, is James' statement, "It is, in short, the re-instatement of the vague to its proper place in our mental life which I am so anxious to press on the attention."[112] Conscious experience is *vague*, in the sense of being richer than an abstract formula. It is unfinished, and here also could be called "vague." Finally, it is as "vague" that consciousness demands selectivity. In brief, conscious experience as an unfinished continuum demands an intense life on the part of each of us, and conscious experience is infinitely rich in the sense of being still in the making, since the last man in experience has not had his say. The net result is an attempt to maintain as much of the richness of life at as intense a level as possible.

THE CONTEXT AS UNFINISHED, UNCERTAIN UNIVERSE

Already implicit in the Jamesian view of consciousness as selective is a view of the universe as uncertain. Just as the selecting aspect of consciousness works within the unfinished context of the stream, so too the human self is free precisely in and through the matrix of experience. One place where James brings this out clearly is in *Pragmatism*:

> To attain perfect clearness in our thought of an object . . . we need only consider what conceivable effects of a practical kind the object may involve — what sensations we are to expect from it, and what reactions we must prepare. Our conception of these effects, whether immediate or remote, is then for us the whole of our conception of the object, as far as that conception has positive significance at all.[113]

As the above text indicates, the meaning of an idea is to be articulated operationally, in terms of its effects. An idea with no effects, or one of no consequence, would be declared meaningless. Any idea, in James' terms, must have its "cash-value"[114] brought out; it must "make a difference."[115] The rationalist thesis that we know reality ahead of time in some *a priori* fashion is rejected. So too is the empiricist thesis that reality consists of a series of atomic units, each self-sufficient and available to the senses. Furthermore, the fact that each and every idea is to be operationally defined asserts that a process is involved. An idea, or a theory, is a project, or hypothesis. In and of itself it is neither true nor false. It becomes true if it can be verified. "Truth," as James said, "*happens* to an idea . . . Its verity *is* in fact an event, a process . . . Its validity is the process of its validation."[116] Thought and action are involved together here. I do not *first* know that an idea is true and then act upon it. Rather only insofar as I act on the idea as a plan do I become aware of its truth or falsity. Action, since it takes place in a context or a situation, is impossible on a private level; it must be public. So part of the verifying process of the idea is its being made public. But this is not the same as saying all ideas must be objectively verified. Such a statement James could not make, since he maintained the efficacy of the human contribution. So, to say that an idea must agree, or lead somewhere useful is not to say that there is an impartial "crucial experiment" which can be performed.

So far, then, we have an epistemological theory which denies the possibility of an absolute, asserts that ideas must be public, though not objective, and steadfastly refuses to set up any one discipline (science, religion, psychology, etc.) as the impartial judge of "making a difference." Is this not subjectivism pure and simple? Cannot one believe anything he wants at any time he wants? Is consciousness efficacious to the point where knowledge is reduced to mere personal whim? The answer to all these questions seems to be "no." True, pragmatism does emphasize the active role each of us plays in any theory of truth:

> What shall we call a thing anyhow? It seems quite arbitrary, for we carve out everything, just as we carve out constellations to suit our human purposes . . . We break the flux of sensible reality into things, . . . at our will. We create the subjects of our true as well as of our false propositions. . . . You can't weed out the human contribution.[118]

Note here the use of the word "create" to emphasize the active role we are all forced to take in structuring experience. Life is intense because man molds it. Any theory will be partially built upon the needs, desires, and interests of its advocates. The so-called "verification" of any idea will include these needs and desires. Impartial verification is, therefore, a myth.

On the other hand, the very fact that all ideas are processes, and as such necessarily involve interpenetrating thought and action, reminds us that, at the very least, ideas must be made public. Here we have an initial hint that we cannot believe anything we want at any time we want. Knowledge, while it is not objective, is more than merely subjective. Any private claim to truth will not be honored; only those that have been made public via action. Action, we remember, has a processive quality to it. It takes time. The theory of truth advocated by James is intensive, but it is also extensive. The process, in other words, of making an idea public is a continuous one, and, more important, it is cumulative:

> Our knowledge grows *in spots* . . . and like grease spots, the spots spread. But we let them spread as little as possible, we keep unaltered as much of our old knowledge, as many of our old prejudices and beliefs, as we can. We patch and tinker more than we renew. The novelty soaks in; it stains the ancient mass; but it is also tinged by what absorbs it. Our past apperceives and cooperates; and in the new equilibrium in which each step forward in the process of learning terminates, it happens relatively seldom that the new fact is added raw. More usually it is embedded cooked, as one might say, or stewed down in the sauce of the old.
>
> New truths thus are resultants of new experiences and of old truths combined and mutually modifying one another.[118]

The process of making a difference then, is not an atomistic, day-to-day affair. This is an important point in the classic American philosophic tradition, having been made in different ways by Peirce[119], Dewey[120], and Whitehead,[121] as well as James. While it is true that I am involved in the process, it is also true that the process is both continual and cumulative. Each and every new moment must take the past into account. Older truths are important; we must remain loyal to as many of them as possible.[122] Indeed, the present moment may be described as an attempt to keep as much of the past as possible, while still keeping the novelty of the present situation. "New truth is always a go-between, a smoother-over of transitions. It marries old opinion to new fact, so as ever to show a minimum of jolt, a maximum of continuity."[123] The picture of truth as presented in *Pragmatism* is one of an ever shifting yet cumulative appropriation. Truth defined as "agreeable leading," "grafts itself onto previous truth, modifying it in the process."[124] Ideas must make a difference, and therefore the real datum is this idea-and-this-projected-difference, that idea-and-that-projected-difference, etc. As these glide into the past they serve to modify new data, either negatively or positively. "Making a difference" then, means *more than believing anything I want whenever I want*. It means adopting those ideas as "true" which enable me to preserve as much of the richness of all my past experiences at as intense a level as possible. The pragmatic method involves both intensity *and* extensionality. It cannot be described as objective, since my needs, desires, and emotions must be taken into account. I find myself as a participant *within* the verifying process. But that process, precisely because it is public, cumulative, and continuous, cannot be described as subjective. Knowledge is not a private emotional whim, to be capriciously changed from day to day. John McDermott, one commentator who has caught this particularly well, asserts that the following texts in *Pragmatism* should be taken together: [125]

> In our cognitive as well as in our active life we are creative. We add, both to the subject and to the predicate part of reality. The world stands really malleable, waiting to receive its final touches at our hands. Like the kingdom of heaven, it suffers human violence willingly. Man engenders truth upon it.

> [and] Woe to him whose beliefs play fast and loose with the order which realities follow in his experience; they will lead him nowhere or else make false connections.

Life is intense because we are called upon to create it; experience is unfinished at the present time. Man molds it as an artist molds his medium. But, the molding is cumulative. What I have chosen by my actions yesterday will influence the present situation. Man's decisions are not objective, but neither are they subjective.

Pragmatism as an epistemological outlook demands an unfinished processive universe, in and through which we come to be. An idea must be "othered" and made public via experiment; that can only be accomplished in an unfinished universe. The ambiguity of life compels participation and vice versa.

To be sure, there are problems, at least of omission, in the Jamesian outlook. In general, the most blatant omission, is that of the "social self" or of a "communal" interpretation of life in and through the matrix of experience. At times James realized that pragmatism's demand for the public dimension of an idea and his view of consciousness surrounded by a marginal "more," lead "to the compounding of consciousness," i. e., to the importance of social intersubjectivity. [126] At other times he seems to have missed this point. Here more work remains to be done.

CONCLUSION

Both James and Herzen espouse a philosophy demanding the interpenetration of thought and action (James: pragmatism; Herzen: the philosophy of the act). Both seem, therefore, to have been against "knowledge for the sake of knowledge." Both philosophers realized that some form of "chance" was necessary for the interpenetration of thinking and action, and for the importance of the person. Both realized that an organic unfinished universe was necessary for freedom, Herzen via the influence of Hegel, James via the stream of consciousness theory; but both realized (to different degrees) that organicism is not synonymous with rationality or logic. Rather is the former inclusive of the latter.

Both philosophies continually affirm the efficacy of the human person. The importance of chance, the interpenetration of thought and action, the unfinished universe — all these seem affixed to this theme. The person is not defined exclusively as a political—social animal, though for Herzen this aspect is more important than for James. Neither philosopher deemed it necessary to articulate the person exclusively in terms of a finished social theory.

Both philosophers, having given up objectivity, attempt not to remain the victim of simple subjectivity. Both turn to some extent to a communal interpretation of experience, Herzen in terms of the peasant commune, James in terms of the compounding of consciousness. James' processive viewpoint is neither exclusively objective nor exclusively subjective. More sophisticated, worked out in better detail than Herzen's, it allows for a view of experience beneath the subject-object dichotomy.

Three differences seem apparent between the two philosophers. First of all James' notion of pragmatism is much wider than Herzen's. God can be pragmatically defined as true if He makes a difference. This is an important point: James' view of pragmatism, though more ambiguous, allows for a much more multidimensional development of the theme of "thinking and doing;" it also prevents any one discipline (e. g., politics) from usurping the role of impartial judge of what is pragmatically true.

Secondly, the emotive overtone in the face of ambiguity and uncertainty is often different. Herzen becomes more pessimistic after the 1848 revolutionary failures, James seems to get more and more joyful as he ages.

Lastly, James preserves "the religious dimension." This step may have enabled him to remain less pessimistic, but it did not cost him an active sense of the person. For James, God was no absolute infinite overseer but a finite "fellow traveler." The religious dimension enabled James to articulate in far greater detail than Herzen the importance of the ambiguity of life.

Despite these differences on the issue of freedom James and Herzen had much in common and could serve again as sources of information and inspiration for the present day. At the close of "The Will to Believe" there is a paragraph which might be taken as the optimal view of both James and Herzen regarding life and freedom:

> In all important transactions of life we have to take a leap in the dark. . . We stand on a mountain pass in the midst of whirling snow and blinding mist, through which we get glimpses now and then of paths which may be deceptive. If we stand still we shall be frozen to death. If we take the wrong road we shall be dashed to pieces. We do not certainly know whether there is any right one. What must we do? "Be strong and of a good courage." Act for the best, hope for the best, and take what comes. . . If death ends all, we cannot meet death better.[127]

While James ultimately turned out to be more optimistic than Herzen, nonetheless the text may stand as a shared ideal statement of the radical ambiguity of freedom.

CHAPTER IV

ROYCE AND KHOMYAKOV
ON COMMUNITY AS PROCESS

In the twentieth century with its overemphasis on individualism and technological achievement the importance of community has been sorely neglected. One consistently finds the community described as an "organization" if it
works well mechanically, or as a bureaucracy if it functions poorly. The net
result of this is a loss of material available for us in times of acute cultural
crisis — like the present age.

The case can be made that a different attitude existed in both pre-twentieth-century America and Russia. In both countries a view of life developed
in response to the confrontation of the experience of the land.[128] While the
individual was undoubtedly important and while all thought had to be implemented by action, nonetheless, in both contexts the community had an
important place. Perhaps the two most important spokesmen for the communal were Josiah Royce in America and Alexis Khomyakov in Russia. The
following pages will attempt to show that these two philosophers pointed towards a similar notion of community as a processive, i. e., historical, temporal
force, and of individual self-realization through the community. In addition,
the most serious problem for each is that of letting the "community" be interpreted as a mere concept or abstract idea. While both thinkers are partly
susceptible to this, nonetheless, there is, in germ, a deeper, more powerful
notion of community to be found in each.

JOSIAH ROYCE

Josiah Royce was born in the frontier mining camp of Grass Valley, California in 1855. His first schooling came from his parents, who had come west
in search of gold. After completing school at the University of California in
1875 he received a fellowship to study abroad. Completing his Ph. D. thesis in
1878 at Johns Hopkins University, he was forced to return to California to
teach logic and rhetoric because there were no other jobs available. Fortunately, four years later he was able to get a job at Harvard, where he was a
tremendous success. A long and intimate friendship developed there between
Royce and William James. His first major work, *The Religious Aspect of
Philosophy*, appeared in 1885. This was followed by, among others, *The*

World and the Individual, in 1901, and finally, by *The Problem of Christianity*, published in 1913. In all of these Royce's view of community is to be found, moving from a merely logical concept towards a more organic notion. He died in Cambridge, Massachusetts in 1916.

Royce defines a community as "a being that attempts to accomplish something in time and through the deeds of its members."[129] A community is essentially the product of a time process, that is, it has a past and it will have a future.[130] It was constituted by a number of individual selves, each of whom was able to look beyond the immediacy of the present moment, to extend himself in terms of sharing a common goal or ideal, past or future. For example, "a community constituted by the fact that each of its members accepts, as part of his own individual life and self, the same expected *future* events that each of his fellows accepts, may be called a *community of expectation*, or upon occasion, a *community of hope*."[131] We should note that a community is not a mere mob or an unintentional group or collectivity. Joining a community requires conscious dedication. John Smith puts it this way:

> . . . While Royce sang the praises of true community as the most powerful civilizing force in human life, he was not unmindful of the evils of that degenerate form of community which expresses itself most violently in the form of the "mob" and less obtrusively, though no less destructively, in the form of mere social conformity. True community does not mean an impersonal mass; true individuality does not mean a willful person who, in the drive to realize himself and have his way, becomes the sworn enemy of social co-operation.[132]

Secondly, the community, as essentially temporal and processive, is the bringing forth, the "incarnating" of a shared ideal. As such it requires the interpenetration of longings, thought, and action. The community was not to be seen merely as an abstract concept. "The concept of the community is . . . a practical conception. It involves the idea of deeds done, and ends sought or attained."[133]

Royce's notion of community and his view of an individual self are interdependent. A self is, by its very essence, a being with a past. Each of us goes through life as an "interpreter." We, as individuals, are neither mere data nor abstract conceptions. "A self is a life whose unity and connectedness depend upon some sort of interpretation of plans, of memories, of hopes, and of deeds."[134] The self, like the community, is essentially temporal; each of us is continually assimilating as much of the past as possible, while advancing into the creative novelty of the future. ". . . My idea of myself is an interpretation of my past, — linked also with an interpretation of my hopes and intentions as to my future."[135] Royce actually worked out an entire "epistemology of interpretation" (borrowed in part from Charles Sanders Peirce). Each of us does not merely see or know some object or idea — rather we see a given object (say a rose) *as* "red" *to* some other person. This "handing on" process is essentially triadic and it at once involves the individual in a communal context. Royce goes on to say:

> Interpretation is not only an essentially social process, but also a process which, when once initiated, can be terminated only by an external and arbitrary interruption, such as death or social separation. By itself, the process of interpretation calls, in ideal, for an infinite sequence of interpretations. For every interpretation, being addressed to somebody, demands interpretation from the one to whom it is addressed.[136]

From the above, it can be easily seen that life, in its ideal state, was essentially social for Royce. A person was not merely an individual. Even more strongly put: a person could only become an individual by participating in a community. A man's fortune was not entirely his own. It was intimately concerned with the communal context to which the individual belonged. Royce did not trust the isolated observation of the individual. His devotion to scientific experiment had taught him that even so-called "expert opinions," when taken in isolation, were always unsatisfactory. "When viewed as if I were alone, I, the individual, am not only doomed to failure, but I am lost in folly."[137]

For Royce, in short, the individual and the communal went hand in hand; both were essentially developmental. The community, as processive, preserved itself as both a one (goal) and a many (individuals). Going further, evil can be defined as the refusal to see oneself as having both a past and a future, i. e., as living in the immediacy of the present moment. Evil, in brief, was isolation.

But which community did an individual join, out of all the possible candidates? Royce's answer was his famous principle of "loyalty to loyalty." First, to become a self one had to be loyal to some cause, to interpret the world in some particular fashion, etc. But secondly, one ought to select that particular cause or ideal which would lead to the greatest possible increase of loyalty among men.[138] In his opinion, Christianity emerged as the most consistent endeavor to preserve community and loyalty. He says:

The essential message of Christianity has been the word that the sense of life, the very being of the time process itself, consists in the progressive realization of the universal Community in and through the longings, the vicissitudes, the tragedies, and the triumphs of this process of the temporal world.[139]

While Royce saw the universal community as the essential goal of Christianity, he nonetheless felt that this goal was being sorely neglected, that the various churches were doing little or nothing to bring about "loyalty to loyalty." Belonging to no particular sect himself, he refused to quibble about these, stating that the only "test" for any one of these was whether or not it furthered the principle of loyalty and in so doing unified all mankind. His view of Christology was along the same lines. It too had lost the developmental sense of incarnating the "beloved community" and had been dominated too much by traditional forms. ". . . *The Christology of the future cannot permanently retain the traditional forms which have heretofore dominated the history both of dogma, and of the visible Christian church.*"[140]

So far then Royce's notion of community is worked out in great detail. It is an organic notion, i. e., it allows for the development of the *whole* person. Royce's major weakness, however, may be seen by asking the question "How do the members of the community 'know' that each has accepted or interpreted a particular past or future event in a common way?" The dilemma here is both obvious and serious. If one merely "knows" in the sense of being "rationally conscious of," then the community seems reduced to an idea or an abstract concept. Indeed Royce sometimes speaks in this fashion, as in an above quote (p. 45) where he states that the community is a "practical conception." But it seems obvious that "the idea of practice" is not "practice." On the other hand, Royce at times seems to include much more in his notion of community than mere rationality. He specifically tells us that knowledge of the community is not love of the community,[141] thereby introducing an extra-rational dimension. Again, he insists that a true community is constituted by "those who are artists in some form of cooperation, and whose art constitutes, for each artist, his own ideally extended life. But the life of an artist depends upon his *love* for his art."[142] If Royce chooses this second "interpretation" of community then, to be sure, the community includes more than a mere idea. It also contains beliefs, emotions, longings, etc. But this notion of community would compel Royce to admit that the members of a given community never really "know" completely, that they always take a chance. In short, communities as truly developmental and organic, are hypothetical and uncertain. As such they demand the interpenetration of belief, thought, and action. While this may affect the view of God as "absolute interpreter" which Royce at times seems to want,[143] nonetheless it seems the only way to preserve the processive dimension of community. Finally, it would allow a more personal view of God, emphasizing His historical importance — something Royce himself (at times) wanted. In brief, either "community as idea" and ultimately as abstraction; or community as organic process, involving emotion-thought-action. Both can be found in Royce, but the latter offers more while demanding uncertainty and ambiguity as essential pre-requisites.

ALEXIS KHOMYAKOV

Alexis Khomyakov was born in Moscow on 1st May, 1804. After serving in the army, he resumed the life of an independent Russian landowner. He was almost completely self-educated, with a deep knowledge of theology and German philosophy, as well as of mathematics and several languages. Usually considered the leader of the Slavophile movement, most of his writings are polemical in tone; they include *Russia and the English Church During the Last Fifty Years*, published in 1844–54, and *The Church Is One*, in 1846. Khomyakov died from cholera in 1860.

Although not developed in sufficient detail, nonetheless the notion of community was of great importance to Khomyakov. "*Sobornost*" was a term he chose to indicate his meaning. "Sobor implique l'idée d'assemblée non pas nécessairement réunie dans un lieu quelconque mais existant virtuellement sans réunion formelle. C'est l'unité dans la pluralité."[144] For Khomyakov, the great tragedy of Christianity could be traced to the "fractionalism" of the church. Christianity, in its fullness, proposed the interpenetration of unity and freedom, joined together in the moral law of mutual love. However, the church of Rome had seen unity and freedom as exclusive, and, regarding unity as more important, had relegated freedom to a secondary position.[145] Protestantism had taken the opposite (and equally one-sided) path, i. e., it had sacrificed unity for individual freedom. Khomyakov saw both of these alternatives as unacceptable; Romanism was an "unnatural tyranny" and Protestantism an "unprincipled revolt."[146] He saw that true freedom only came in and through the unity of the community, not in spite of it. On the other hand, he rejected all "authoritarian" attempts at enforcing unity. The Church in its true form was (or should be) "poly-hypostatic" — it is united organically and not externally.[147] No single community or pastor was to be acknowledged as sole custodian of the whole faith of the church.[148] The latter did not have official advocates, and every member of the church formed an organic part of it.

Like Royce, Khomyakov thought the Christian tradition to be of utmost importance. Man was essentially a social animal; he could only survive by mutual love, by upholding the one-among-many doctrine of the community.

> A man, however, does not find in the Church something foreign to himself. He finds himself in it, himself not in the impotence of spiritual solitude, but in the might of his spiritual, sincere union with his brothers, with his Saviour. He finds himself in it in his perfection, or rather, he finds in it that which is perfect in himself, the Divine inspiration which constantly evaporates in the crude impunity of every separate, individual existence.[149]

Khomyakov developed what Zenkovsky calls a social theory of knowledge, or a "collective epistemology."[150] Truth is inaccessible to the isolated individual, but it is accessible to a group of thinkers bound together by love. "Rationalism" is abstract logical knowledge, mere externality, separated from the moral principle. The higher intellect (*razum*) flourishes only in friendly communion with other thinking beings. It is the lower intellect (*rassudok*) which engages in private analysis and does not inquire communally. As Zenkovsky notes, the Kantian distinction between *Verstand* (purely logical operations) and *Vernunft*, as a source of ideas, was very influential here. However, in Khomyakov the Kantian division between rationality and "total reason" is merged with the Slavophile distinction between rational knowledge and "faith."[151]

"Christian knowledge is a matter not of intellectual investigation, but of a living faith."[152] Pure analytical thought therefore, taken by itself, is the fruit of an impoverished and egotistical soul.[153] Evil for Khomyakov, as for Royce, was primarily a form of isolationism. Man is evil precisely insofar as he isolates himself from the community through the exclusive use of mere reason.

As with Royce, however, one could ask the question: "How does a person 'know' that he is in the community?" or "How does a person 'know that the knows' what is accessible only to the community? "

Here again the alternatives would seem to be: either the members of the community "know" it as a mere concept or idea; or the members of the community never know "for sure," but act rather on the hypothesis of faith. Hence there would be more to the community than the mere idea of community; the community, *qua* hypothesis, would have to take place in time, to involve the interpenetration of thinking and doing, thought and action. There are occasional hints in Khomyakov's texts that he wants to get beyond the mere idea of community,[154] that he seeks awareness of a world beneath that of mere logical analysis. However, his view that the true Christian life is interior prevents him from developing a truly processive view of community.

> L'unité intérieure et vraie, produit et manifestation de la liberté, l'unité basée non sur science rationaliste ni sur une convention arbitraire, mais sur la loi morale de l'amour mutuel . . . telle est l'unité de l'Eglise.[155]

By choosing one category over another here, Khomyakov emphasizes the internal, leaving little room for the translation of thought into action. This was Royce's problem also. If time is reduced to a mere category, the truly processive sense of cummunity cannot come to be. In general Khomyakov wavers between adopting an alternative set of categories to those he found wanting, and rejecting both sets of categories as inadequate. As seen above, some of Khomyakov's writings show the Roman Church as rationalistic, viewing freedom and unity as exclusive and selecting one of them.[156] Hence we have "the external," "the authoritative 'one' " and "the rationalistic" somehow connected. Opposing there are, it would seem, "the interior," "the decentralized 'many' " and "the irrational." Khomyakov was perceptive enough to see that freedom and unity could not be separated, that a person becomes a unique individual through "the many." He also, as Zenkovsky has pointed out, rejected both mere rationalism and mere irrationalism.

> He once came out sharply against irrationalism, in which he saw an extreme opposite to the other extreme of rationalism. "Let us leave," he wrote "to the despair of some Western people, frightened by the suicidal development of rationalism, the blind and partly feigned contempt for science.[157]

Unfortunately, however, the one dichotomy he does not clearly reject is the internal/external. By identifying the "really real" world with the interior he de-emphasizes the interpenetration of thought and action and runs the risk of seeing all process as merely an idea. His de-emphasis of the importance of actualization leads him to accord only secondary importance to the historical dimension of Christ.[158] Although God revealed himself to all creatures as a unique moral Being in the son of man, Jesus, nonetheless this is only historical revelation. "La révélation du fils de l'homme, qui a surgi sur la face mobile des siècles, c'est encore la pensée éternelle de Dieu."[159] Again, this position runs the risk of losing an organic sense of time, reducing it to a mere idea or concept, and allowing no way to deal with the "problem of evil" — mainly because the latter is conquered from all time in the very thought of Christ.[160]

In brief, a truly organic sense of community must allow for individual self-development in and through an organic context. This necessitates the interpenetration of thought and action. Khomyakov begins the long process of working out the notion of community. He rejects *both* terms of several sets of categories. But he maintains the internal and thus runs the risk of relegating action and development to secondary or non-existent status.[161] This would ultimately result in the community becoming a mere concept or idea — something Khomyakov himself would have rejected.

In closing, it would seem that the notion of community is essentially a processive one. It involves the interpenetration of belief, thought and action. As such a community is essentially mysterious or ambiguous. The members of a community must always run a risk. On the other hand this risk is not purely irrational. Rather does their commitment become more or less justified as the community is incarnated in time. The community can be pointed towards or called into being via persuasive reasoning, but not demonstrated or "solved" as a problem. Time must be seen as a matrix in and through which the community comes to be. Both Royce and Khomyakov struggled to maintain this mysterious, developmental sense of community. Although not entirely successful, both could again serve as models for present-day reconstructions of community.

CHAPTER V

ART VS. SCIENCE
IN DEWEY AND CHERNYSHEVSKY

In the latter part of the nineteenth century, both Russia and America became fascinated with "science." The scientific outlook was one natural outgrowth of a culture suspicious of *a priori* deductive systems — of "reason for the sake of reason."[162] However, in both countries this fascination with science sometimes resulted in the downplaying of other dimensions of experience, i. e., the aesthetic.

In the present chapter we shall compare the scientific and the aesthetic views of John Dewey and Nicholas Chernyshevsky. Though Dewey's outlook is undoubtedly more profound and far-reaching than that of Chernyshevsky, nonetheless both views come dangerously close to identifying science and art as one and the same thing, or worse, making art the handmaiden of science.

DEWEY ON ART AND SCIENCE

John Dewey (1859–1952) was born in Burlington, Vermont and did his studies at the University of Vermont and at Johns Hopkins University. He taught at universities in Michigan, Minnesota, Chicago and New York. He is known for his doctrine of instrumentalism and for the effect that he had on theories of education around the world. He began his philosophical career under the influence of Hegel, only to move later to a naturalism of organism and environment. He was a profilic writer. Among his most famous works: *Experience and Nature, Reconstruction in Philosophy, Individualism Old and New, Art as Experience*. The last is usually considered to be one of the truly great recent contributions to aesthetic theory.

Dewey tells us at the very beginning of *Art as Experience* that he wishes to arrive at his theory of art by means of a detour. In his opinion, life and art had been disassociated for too long, and he wished to restore continuity between them. "Life," for Dewey, "goes on in an environment; not merely *in* it but because of it, through interaction with it."[163] An individual organism comes to be by falling out of the flux of experience in some respect; it copes with the challenge or confrontation by utilizing his funded past experience, returning then to experience in a richer, more meaningful manner. "Life grows when a temporary falling out is a transition to a more extensive balance of the energies of the organism with those of the conditions under which it lives."[164] Each of us then is continually on a journey; we are in the process of making ourselves in and through the matrix of experience. Most importantly, because "experience is the fulfillment of an organism in its struggles and achievements in a world of things, it is art in germ."[165] More specifically, an aesthetic experience is one which runs its course to fulfillment. The organism is confronted by something and manages to draw upon its past so as to transform the confrontation into a highly participatory experience. In an aesthetic expereience then, there is a cumulative sense, i. e., a certain tempo and a consummatory moment toward the end, when the organism assembles everything in a satisfying manner.

That which distinguishes an experience as aesthetic is conversion of resistance and tensions, of excitations that in themselves are temptations to diversion, into a movement toward an inclusive and fulfilling close.[166]

Since experience is essentially temporal, it follows that art, being a heightened form of experience, is itself a process. Dewey distinguishes clearly between a product of art and a work of art:

The *product* of art — temple, painting, statue, poem — is not the *work* of art. The work takes place when a human being co-operates with the product so that the outcome is an experience that is enjoyed because of its liberating and ordered properties.[167]

The above picture is a very democratic view of art; it does not recognize a complete distinction between the fine arts and the practical arts. Unlike some theories of formalism, it does not view art as dealing with a "higher" geometric realm. Unlike some imitation theories, it does not divide existence into nature and its pale artistic reproductions. Almost anything could (given the unfinished processive universe) be raised to the status of art. So too, any growing individual is by definition an artist (potentially). Why then has this not been recognized long before? Dewey's answer is that the role art plays in civilization is influenced by its relationship to science and to the social ramifications of industry.

The mechanical stands at the pole opposite to that of the esthetic, and production of goods is now mechanical. The liberty of choice allowed to the craftsman who worked by hand has almost vanished with the general use of the machine. Production of objects enjoyed in direct experience by those who possess, to some extent, the capacity to produce useful commodities expressing individual values, has become a specialized matter apart from the general run of production. This fact is probably the most important factor in the status of art in present civilization.[168]

Dewey's view of art, then, as a "participatory celebration of experience," has definite social and moral dimensions. As we might expect, experience, as unfinished and ambiguous, is fundamentally available, "disponible"[169] — anyone can (or should be able to) create in and through the matrix of experience. But this is not so. The worker has been shut off. For aesthetic reasons, then, a radical social alteration is necessary, one which would allow the worker more participation in his product. In this scenario Dewey sees the machine itself as neutral — it does not obstruct the worker's enjoyment in work well done. Rather

> oligarchical control from the outside of the processes and the products of work is the chief force in preventing the worker from having that intimate interest in what he does and makes that is an essential prerequisite of aesthetic satisfaction.[170]

The remedy then consists in changing the social structure. How does one do this? Apparently by extending the method of science to other areas of experience, i. e., the social and the economic. Although the machine is neutral, the scientific method is positive.

> ... in doing their specific jobs scientific men worked out a method of inquiry so inclusive in range and so penetrating, so pervasive and so universal, as to provide the pattern and model which permits, invites and even demands the kind of formulation that falls within the function of philosophy. It is a method of knowing that is self-corrective in operation; that learns from failures as from successes. The heart of the method is the discovery of the identity of inquiry with discovery.[171]

In *Reconstruction in Philosophy* Dewey attempted to depict the change between the classical model of the universe and the newer, more "scientific" model. The old view of the universe was essence-oriented, focused on a supernatural world, was past rather than future oriented, and advocated the divorce of the contemplative and the practical.[172] For Dewey, matters began to change with Francis Bacon. Heralding Bacon as the harbinger of the new approach to the universe, Dewey goes on to unpack the method of science as essentially future- rather than past-oriented, more interested in the processive than the permanent or fixed, and demanding the fusion of thought and action. Thinking now has the form of hypothesis, and no scientist really knows what he thinks until he experiments in his laboratory. Lastly, no one scientist can do all of the thinking. Since what I think is unclear until I act and since how you act changes me by changing the context in and through which I come to be (in this case a scientist) the scientific method is essentially communal. This mode of approach is essentially anti-Cartesian. It does not view the individual knower as existing apart from contemporaries. In addition, it rejects the view that *a priori* deductive knowledge is possible. Just as clearly, however, it rejects the empiricist position that only that which is immediately present (and hence atemporal) is real.

This view of science, like Dewey's view of art, is essentially ongoing and growth-oriented. Any interruption of the process of science is to be viewed as both unscientific and ugly (non-aesthetic). The political-economic situation in capitalism is one in which the democratic atmosphere of both art and science is curtailed. Viewing the individual as an isolated unit who exists in spite of context and of others, and viewing economics in a *laissez faire* manner are two ways of bifurcating experience. Experience in its basic state is essentially organic and processive — it can be dealt with most adequately via the method of science. In short, political and economic evils will go away if one practices this method of science more consistently.

Science then is a continually changing process, in which the organism comes to grips with an issue, draws on his past, and tries to assemble everything and return to experience. Ironically, then, the process of science and the process of art seem to be the same for Dewey. He seems not to like this result, and several times tries to re-introduce some distinction. For example, in *Experience and Nature* he tells us that

> . . . science is an art, art is practice, and . . . the only distinction worth drawing is not between practice and theory, but between those modes of practice that are not intelligent, not inherently and immediately enjoyable, and those which are full of enjoyed meanings. When this perception dawns, it will be a commonplace that art — the mode of activity that is charged with meanings capable of immediately enjoyed possession — is the complete culmination of nature, and that "science" is properly a handmaiden that conducts natural events to this happy issue.[173]

Again, in *Art as Experience* he says that "Science states meanings; art expresses them."[174] Here however, he seems to be arguing against one of his own theses. Both art and science are processes. A scientific statement is analogous to a *product* of art — not the *work* of art. So the work of art should be compared to the scientific procedure. Professor Gauss has caught this point well:

> The painted picture, the physical sounds of music, the printed works of poetry are . . . physical vehicles. They too, as they stand are merely directions for producing experiences. They are simply plain statements, cues to tell us, the spectators, how to operate. On the other hand the scientific statement as a direction for producing something is a direction for how one attains an experience . . . We moderns do not think of science so much as a set of statements as we do as a procedure. As such, I reiterate, it is consummate artistry. It fits exactly Dewey's definition of fine art as "an organization of energies to move cumulatively to a terminal whole in which the values of all means and media are incorporated."[175]

In sum, the process of art, which is an intensification of ordinary experience, has been eroded by social conditions. The process of science, which Dewey wanted to extend into more and more areas of thought, is either the handmaiden to art, or art and science are identical processes. Science and art seem to be similar; at least Dewey has difficulty distinguishing them. He seems to be saying that the more scientific/aesthetic we are, the better the world will be socially and politically.

However, it would seem that something is wrong here. We have become far more scientific since Dewey wrote this work and yet few would accuse us of becoming more aesthetic. If anything there seems to be a loss of the aesthetic dimension in our contemporary era. Indeed even Dewey seems to glimpse a danger here, since he pulls back at times from identifying science and art. Is there, then, anything that does distinguish art from science?

Here Dewey made a fundamental mistake. He had the beginnings of a distinction, but chose not to emphasize it. Specifically, Dewey began to lose track of the importance of vagueness or ambiguity. The difference between art and science is not adequately stated in terms of immediate expression (art) vs. mediated statements (science). Rather is ambiguity or vagueness a fundamental characteristic of any great "art process." One is "condemned" to be an artist only in a vague or mysterious or uncertain situation. In *Art as Experience* Dewey notes that

> About every explicit and focal object there is a recession into the implicit which is not intellectually grasped. In reflection we call it dim and vague. But in the original experience it is not identified as the vague. It is a function of the whole situation, and not an element in it, as it would have to be in order to be apprehended *as* vague.[176]

Dewey here clearly recognizes the foreground/background construction of all objects of perception. He realizes that this vague sense of a "more" existing on the periphery is unavoidable. But he does not see the possibility of the vagueness existing on different levels of perception, or even containing different modes within a single perception. In *Experience and Nature* he comes closer to this, when he tells us that experience, as both process and product, occurs when

> activity is productive of an object that affords continuously renewed delight. This condition requires that the object be, with its successive consequences, indefinitely instrumental to new satisfying events. For otherwise the object is quickly exhausted and satiety sets in. Anyone, who reflects upon the commonplace that a measure of artistic products is their capacity to attract and retain observation with satisfaction under whatever conditions they are approached, while things of less quality soon lose capacity to hold attention, becoming indifferent or repellent upon subsequent approach, has a sure demonstration that a genuinely aesthetic object is not exclusively consummatory, but is causally productive as well. A consummatory object that is not also instrumental turns in time to the dust and ashes of boredom. The "eternal" quality of great art is its renewed instrumentality for further consummatory experiences.[177]

This and other passages indicate that for Dewey vagueness or mystery, in the sense of capacity for continual re-interpretation, is an essential characteristic of art. Maybe the only essential trait. For renewed instrumentality implies indefiniteness both as to uses and to users. It is *not* the goal of science to preserve vagueness or ambiguity but in some sense to clear it up. A work of art must be essentially mysterious in order for the process of art to be truly ongoing. Some artists are manifestly better at incorporating vagueness than others. Vagueness is not intentional obfuscation. Nor is it to be seen as "I don't understand it, therefore it must be good." Rather vagueness refers to the ability of a piece of art to deal on many different levels of experience simultaneously without reducing these to any one or two levels. This seems to be a criterion or a goal of art which is neither a criterion nor a goal in science. Dewey gives some hints that he recognizes this distinction in the above quotes, but his realization is neither clear nor steadfast. Usually art and science are seen as highly similar if not identical.

CHERNYSHEVSKY ON ART AND SCIENCE

Nicholas Gavrilovich Chernyshevsky was born in Saratov in 1828. Educated first at home until he was sixteen, he then graduated from the Theological Seminary, then from St. Petersburg University. It was during his university years that Chernyshevsky formulated his social and political outlook. While teaching in a gymnasium in Saratov, Chernyshevsky also found time to pass his Master's examination in Russian literature with a thesis on "The Aesthetic Relations of Art to Reality". His involvement with the journal *Sovremennik* ('The Contemporary') dates from 1853 and he quickly rose to the position of spokesman for radical thought. Arrested for political activity in 1862, Chernyshevsky was sentenced to exile in Siberia. He was permitted to return to Russia in 1883, and only in 1888 was he allowed to return to Saratov. By then in bad health, he died in Saratov in 1889.

At the very beginning of "The Aesthetic Relations of Art to Reality" Chernyshevsky announces his fascination with "science."

> Respect for real life, distrust of a priori hypotheses, . . . such is the character of the trend that now predominates in science. The author is of the opinion that our aesthetic convictions, if it is still worth our while to discuss aesthetics, should also be brought into line with this.[178]

Current aesthetic theory was much too idealistic; it viewed physical reality as a second-rate experience and a work of art as worthy only if it represented a higher transcendental region. Current idealistic aesthetics, in his opinion, viewed art as originating in an "irresistible striving for beauty which, unsatisfied by anything in objective reality, leads man to create artificial embodiments of true beauty."[179] While Chernyshevsky agreed with the view that art was a substitute for reality, he did not agree that it was superior. So in direct "opposition" to idealism, Chernyshevsky holds that the dearest thing in the world is life.[180] Therefore true beauty resides in this real physical world. "Beautiful is the object which expresses life, or reminds us of life."[181] "Life" here refers to individual existence; generality as such is an illusion.

> . . . The definition "beauty is life," makes it clear why there are no abstract ideas, but only individual beings in the sphere of beauty — we see life only in real living beings; abstract, general ideas do not enter the sphere of life.[182]

Apparently then, the primary essence of a work of art is to point beyond itself. Chernyshevsky disagrees with the idealists on where it points — not up toward a perfect Platonic realm. This (Platonic) move implies that the world we are in is flawed and not worthy of consideration. Rather is the work of art to point back towards the real "scientific" world. "The first object of art is to reproduce reality."[183] Going further, a work of art is always second-rate when compared with reality. "We . . . assert that art cannot stand comparison with living reality and completely lacks the virility that reality possesses; we regard this as being beyond doubt."[184]

At times, Chernyshevsky seems to believe that this position denies any substantive reality to the work of art itself. He tells us that the so-called "creative imagination" of the artist is extremely limited; that the role of the artist is one of combining various impressions which are received from experience. The artist's imagination only serves to diversify an object. The imagination may magnify an object received; however it is impossible to imagine anything which has not been observed or experienced.[185] Again, he states that the imagination cannot "picture a rose better than the rose in nature."[186] This position seems consistent with Chernyshevsky's view that man does not have a dualistic nature. He contains no separate spirit or mind not derivable from external nature. Hence, once again when philosophy deals with human issues it is based on the natural sciences. Philosophy must view the human being in the same fashion as medicine, physiology and chemistry. These sciences, he believes, have already demonstrated the impossibility of a dualistic approach to man. Philosophy has added the final capstone, noting that if another nature existed in the human being, it would reveal itself in some fashion. Since this has not occurred, the non-duality of human existence is beyond doubt.[187]

Since the real world is made up of particulars and since aesthetic imagination or creative spirit is not a separate element, the work of art *qua* reproduction "must contain as little of the abstract as possible; everything in it must be, as far as possible, expressed concretely in living scenes and in individual images."[188] However, in other texts he seems to tell us that a work of art, *qua* representation, is necessarily general.

> The power of art particularly of poetry is usually the power to awaken memory. Because of its very incompleteness, indefiniteness, precisely because it is usually only a "generalization," and not a living individual image or event, a work of art is particularly capable of awakening our memory.[189]

In his work on "The Poetics of Aristotle", he is even less consistent. Confronted with the famous Aristotelian distinction between poetry and history, Chernyshevsky oscillates between admitting that "poetry depicts not petty details, but that which is general and characteristic"[190] and trying to explain this by saying that actual events proceed from general necessity.

> Poetry [for Aristotle] demands that the details of the action should necessarily flow one from the other, and that their concatenation should seem probable. Nothing prevents some actual events from satisfying this demand; everything in them developed of necessity, and everything is probable — why, then, should not the poet take them in their true form?[191]

This position seems to say that there is a general law present in nature and that a work of art somehow "reproduces" this general law. It seems directly contradictory to the thesis that the really real is the individual and that art must imitate the singular. This second group of texts seems to give art a more active role, i. e., they seem to indicate that art adds something to reality (since apparently not all actual events "developed of necessity" and the artist had to select).

There is a second aspect of Chernyshevsky's theory of art which seems inconsistent with a work being a mere reproduction, namely, when he further stipulates *what* from life is to be reproduced:

> The essential purpose of art is to reproduce *what is of interest to man* in real life. But, being interested in the phenomena of life, man cannot but, consciously or unconsciously, pronounce judgment on them. The poet, or artist, being unable to cease to be a man, cannot, even if he wanted to, refrain from pronouncing judgment on the phenomena he depicts. This judgment is expressed in his work — this is another purpose of art, which places it among the moral activities of man.[192]

Leaving aside how one unconsciously pronounces judgment, this position clearly gives an active role to the work of art. A painting or a poem is a moral judgment on reality, not merely a copy. And how are moral judgments made? Elsewhere Chernyshevsky tells us that we are guided by the pleasure principle in morals. Ethically, human beings are egoists; good is defined in terms of utilitarian self-interest, or, the good is the desirable.[193] Chernyshevsky goes on to distinguish immediate from long-range pleasures[194] and asserts that "the interests of mankind as a whole stand higher than the interests of an individual nation."[195] Morality is a science, less advanced than natural science,[196] but nonetheless a science. Furthermore,

> science deals with nations, not with an individual man; with man, but not with a Frenchman or Englishman, not with the merchant or the bureau-

crat. Science recognizes as truth only that which constitutes human nature. Only that which is useful to man in general is regarded as true good.[197]

Here it would seem indeed that the whole is greater than the sum of its parts. Applying this to a theory of art, which we remember is trying to become more "scientific," we have something like the following: art imitates what man finds pleasing. But what men in general find pleasing is better than what you or I find pleasing. This would seem to militate again towards art dealing with the essential rather than the individual. Furthermore, it entails admitting either that all things are pleasing but some things are more pleasing than others, or that some things are ugly. Chernyshevsky chooses the latter version, asserting that the really practical person gives up dreams out of tune with nature's laws. However, this same practical fellow realizes that much in reality is not beautiful but ugly, and he strives to combat and overcome these elements in order to bring about human well-being.[198]

The idea of art being an impartial copy either of a particular or of a general essence seems then to have disappeared. A poem or picture is a moral judgment of the general conditions which do exist *vis à vis* what they might be. "Art for art's sake" is an unacceptable notion, as unacceptable as "science for science's sake." All human activity must have some function; otherwise it is merely fruitless pleasure, a useless and idle occupation.[199]

And what is the peculiar quality of art if it is apparently neither mere imitation nor mere pleasure? Art is *infectious*; it can popularize or make available to the masses the results of scientific procedure.

> . . . it must be admitted that it [art] very successfully attracts an enormous mass of people, and thereby unintentionally helps to spread education, a clear conception of things – everything which is of intellectual, and therefore, of subsequent material benefit to the people. Art, or it would be better to say poetry (only poetry, for the other arts do very little in this respect), spreads among the mass of the reading public an enormous amount of knowledge and, what is still more important, familiarizes them with the concepts worked out by science – such is poetry's great purpose in life.[200]

Art then is the handmaiden of science; this is its essential purpose.

Science is the repository of the experience and reflections of the human race; and it is chiefly on the basis of science that people's conceptions, and subsequently their morals and lives, are improved. But the discoveries and deductions of science are really beneficial only when they spread among the mass of the public. Science is stern and forbidding in its original shape; it does not attract the crowd. Science demands of its followers a vast amount of preliminary knowledge and, what is even more rarely met with among the majority, the habit of serious thinking. Therefore, to permeate the masses, science must divest itself of scientific form . . . This palatable reading is provided by novels, stories, etc. [201]

Apparently then art does something that science cannot do; it fosters understanding and perhaps dreams on a broad scale. Both art and science are textbooks, studies of reality. It follows that, just as science makes no claim to stand above reality, so too art must make no such claim. [202]

In summary then, we have the following: art, which usually means poetry for Chernyshevsky, reproduces this life, not one "up there."

But then a turn is made. Art produces not the particulars of this life but the essential idea in this life. Apparently there is more than one essential idea of this life, for Chernyshevsky sees the work of art as reproducing the essential ideal of this life. Art's real importance then comes from popularizing dreaming. Art unfreezes things insofar as it is infectious. Art itself does not foster dreaming (or a better world); this task is left for science.

The final court of appeal then turns out to be science, which is interested in improving people's lives. This might be allowed, but only if it were shown that science really had some claim to be the true foundation. Defining science as "the repository of the experience and reflections of the human race" is so nebulous as to offer little or nothing in that direction. If one takes the other tack and asserts that by science Chernyshevsky meant "materialism" then one is left with the paradox that Chernyshevsky was consistently inconsistent in carrying out the implications of his theory. As William Woehrlin notes:

There is no doubt that Chernyshevskii's materialistic monism helped him, as it did writers of the French Enlightenment, to mount an attack on the past. With its use, many traditional ideals and values that could not be derived scientifically from nature were automatically declared invalid, and the slate rubbed clean to start afresh . . . Nevertheless, when Chernyshevskii made his criticisms, and especially when he looked to the future, despite the scientific cast of his statements, he implied values that did not stem directly or necessarily from his basic materialistic philosophy. And when his thought led him to choose between consistency of argument and personally cherished values and aspirations, he clearly preferred the latter. [203]

A more serious problem than that of mere inconsistency is involved here. The foreground/background construction of a painting, the ongoing focus/fringe continuum, the ability for the same or different people to "see" different aspects of a work at different times — all these factors militate toward a view of art as inherently ambiguous. Conversely, because art presents itself in this multilayered ambiguous fashion it compels a commitment or response on the part of the viewer. In this it functions in the same way as dreaming. For one only dreams or wonders in an uncertain or vague situation — one which admits of several posibilities. The thesis that art, which fosters dreaming, is essentially ambiguous and that this is good, seems either missed or underplayed by Chernyshevsky. Caught up in responding to idealism by espousing a realist approach to art, Chernyshevsky misses the possibility that art, unlike science, may not solve problems (or not only do so) but may indeed have as its purpose the reaffirmation of the vague. E. Lampert expresses this point well:

> It is not difficult to see the limitations of this "objective," "realist" approach to art. It may induce not only an interest in things said or represented at the expense of the way in which they are said or represented. It may cause, above all, an underestimation of sensibility and imagination. We need the contrasts of absolute and relative values, of idea and reality, fantasy and result, poetry and action, detachment and intimacy. They supply the element of tension in art as in life, allowing things and people to be mysterious and surprising, as, in fact, they mostly are. "L'art est fait pour troubler: la science rassure."[204]

CONCLUSION

Both Chernyshevsky and Dewey rejected the bifurcation of experience. Both wanted to obliterate a transcendental view of art and replace it with one affirming the close connection of art and ordinary life. Both philosophers stress the close connection of art and science.

Dewey thinks science to be the handmaiden of art but art and science turn out to be the same process. Various texts in his work indicate an ability to accept the essential vagueness or ambiguity of a work of art. But usually art and science seem highly similar, if not identical. Dewey seems afraid of this,

and at times catches glimpses of the possibility of art reintroducing or up-
grading vagueness rather than obliterating it.

Chernyshevsky thinks art to be the handmaiden of science. His definition
of science is so wide as to render this claim unanalyzable. If science is taken
as deterministic materialism, art as its pale reflection is anything but ambiguous. Chernyshevsky too seems to be afraid of this conclusion at times. The
closest he comes to recognizing that art adds something not given in science
seems to be his view that art is infectious or permeating. But the possibility of
art being infectious at various different levels, in different ways, and therefore
being essentially vague, seems to be one he was ultimately not willing to
admit.

The infectious quality of art is also highlighted by John Dewey. In the
aesthetic process, the product of art is continually reinterpreted by future
onlookers. The possibility of a work of art being cumulative/consummatory
in various ways at various levels seems much more likely in Dewey than in
Chernyshevsky. Why it is more likely is a difficult question. But one could
suspect that at the very end, art is closer to the fundamental uncertainty and
ambiguity of experience than science is. Experience was not uncertain in
Chernyshevsky. It was either blatantly stultifying through political pressure,
or utopian in the sense of what was ultimately not to be. For Dewey (at his
best) these would be ideal limit cases, and his view of art could more easily
deal with the real world of what "is for the present but might change in a
moment, to be followed by something else," and so on and so on. This seems
closer to where real ambiguity lies, although Dewey himself seems ambivalent
as to whether to celebrate the ambiguity of life or to control and manipulate
it.

CHAPTER VI

UNDERLYING THEMES
AND THE PRESENT CULTURAL CONTEXT

Although each is difficult to characterize in complete fashion, nonetheless both the Russian and American contexts exhibit strikingly similar themes in their pre-twentieth-century development. While no complete identity is asserted, the following six characteristics seem to be the most pervasive.

THE REVOLT AGAINST CARTESIANISM

This theme is a common one in both Russian and American thought. The Cartesian position advocated a view of the human person as a detached spectator. The *cogito* was pure thought, having nothing to do with action, and hopefully not overly influenced by will. The universe which the cogito peered out at was a tidy geometric one; only those things were real which could be quantified. A neat and strict "in here"—"out there" dualism was adopted, distinguishing clearly and distinctly mind and body, self and world. Such a view relegates the paradoxes of the universe and of history to the stage of being illusions, and offers no "space of operation" for human activity.

Both the Russian and the American traditions found this outlook abstract and misleading. James, for example, saw the human being not as a spectator but as a participator; Royce's idealism saw the person as an interpreter — a transformer of experiences, not a mere photo-copier. Dewey's view lies in the same vein; the human being is a creature who becomes conscious in the act of being confronted by experience and coming to grips with this confrontation in a satisfactory manner.

From the Russian side, Herzen's philosophy of the act rejected the self-sufficiency of pure thought. Chernyshevsky's fascination with science was based, however insufficiently, on the belief that science led to the embodiment of thought in action. Chaadayev was dedicated to incarnating the idea of God on earth.

In place of the Cartesian view of the universe, then, we are given an embodied subject; in place of the finished and a-historical universe of gemoetry we are offered an unfinished context. The dualism of self and world is rejected, and in its place is posited a more involved picture of the human being as active in the universe.

THE HUMAN BEING AS PARTICIPATOR

This theme also occupies an important place in both traditions. Once the Cartesian subject is banished, the way is open for a new view of the person. The new view is one which compels commitment and participation on the part of each individual. A person does not find himself outside the sphere of the universe, but rather within the circle. The human contribution cannot be weeded out, as James would say. For Dewey, all people are potentially artists, and the world is ultimately a work of art. Try as we may we cannot avoid the responsibility of adding the final touches to the unfinished universe.

To be sure, great differences remained between the two traditions and indeed among the members of each side as to how much freedom or what kind of participation actually existed or was necessary. For Emerson, Chaadayev, Khomyakov and Royce, the activity of the human being seems to be essentially religious. It always involves in some fashion the co-creative aspect of building the kingdom of Zion on earth. The question of the political realm is not adequately dealt with, though it sometimes appears in a none too pretty fashion. Emerson, as we know, was upset about slavery, but saw the human being's activity on a more religious level. Royce, though advocating the importance of activity in *The Problem of Christianity*, was completely upset and dismayed by the oncoming First World War. Chaadayev was the personal victim of a conservative political context and Khomyakov, perhaps the unwitting victim of a tightening of the political reins, articulates a view in which he seems afraid to allow too much activity to the human person. Perhaps in the Russian situation the very impossibility of political activity acted as a catalyst toward seeing human activity as religious. Nonetheless, Herzen's views on the human as a doer are clearly political though they become pessimistic; James clearly viewed the human as a doer but whether of an essentially religious or political nature seems difficult to decide. There is of course "the moral equivalent of war;" on the other hand the last lecture of *Pragmatism* and also *A Pluralistic Universe* make clear how important the religious dimension was to James, and within it, the view of man as co-creator.

With all these differences, it remains clear nonetheless that these two traditions viewed the human being as a maker or an artist, not merely a detached thinker. They disagreed on whether his activity was political or religious, or both, but they consistently upheld the view that some type or types of activity could make a difference in the universe — even if only a small one.

THE CONTEXT: AN UNFINISHED, MYSTERIOUS UNIVERSE

Human activity can only make a difference if the universe is unfinished, at least in some sense. Otherwise our actions may look efficacious enough but in the long run activity appears as merely illusory. Again, to a greater or lesser extent, the thinkers on both sides of the ocean upheld the unfinished character of everything. Objectivity — in the sense of a final outlook already in hand, was rejected. The activity of the human subject was important precisely because objectivity could not be found or deduced. (The question of the restraints on human subjectivity given the loss of objectivity will be taken up in the two last sections of this chapter). In the American tradition this theme is clear, and it is repeated again and again by its foremost spokesmen. The universe is no longer a tidy spot, Dewey tells us in *Reconstruction in Philosophy*; growth is the only moral absolute. James continually wants to reintroduce the vague to its proper place in our experience. He thought the universe to be wild — "game-flavored as a hawk's wing. Nature is miracle all; and the same returns not save to bring the different."[205] In a less radical vein, Royce saw the fundamental human activity to be that of interpreting an uncertain context. The world did not present itself as a billboard to be read off, but rather as a paradox to be interpreted in an ongoing fashion through symbols. Every single thing in nature for Emerson was paradoxical — a leaf could be seen in two ways — as an individual entity, or as the focalization of divinity. In other words, as a leaf (or as a universe) it was ambiguous.

The Russians too saw the universe as mysterious, though in differing degrees. Herzen believed that nature had only given vague hints as to her intentions, and that the rest was left to the human being as doer. Chaadayev believed in Providence, but thought the details were vague enough to allow for human activity. Chernyshevsky professed to believe in materialism, but his activity itself indicates how uncertain he thought things to be, and how much he could dream.

Again, to be sure, differences exist here. Most of the thinkers interested primarily in religion shy away from making the universe appear too ambiguous — that would ultimately limit God's power too much. Also, it must be said that the ambiguity of nature is heralded much more in the Amterican tradition. It is probably all one can do to find novelty and ambiguity in a tsarist-dominated context, whereas in America as Boorstin noted, it took effort to avoid novelty. Nonetheless, both traditions did find the universe to be more ambiguous than it was usually deemed to be, and both, to an extent, realized the importance of that ambiguity.

THE INTERPENETRATION OF THOUGHT AND ACTION

With the universe seen as unfinished and the human being as a participator, all thoughts become "plans of action." No *a priori* deductive system was deemed self-sufficient. Reason was seen as important only insofar as truths could be embodied. Ideas then are hypotheses for James. An idea becomes true insofar as it is incarnated in experience, insofar as it leads the person having the idea into better and better relations with experience. The subject/object dichotomy of traditional epistemology is cast off and in its place a philosophy of interaction is advocated. This may be termed "pragmatism" — but only if the term is used in its widest possible sense. God can be pragmatically defined as true for James, if the idea of Divinity makes a difference in our lives. So too Emerson tells us that he only knows what he has undergone — what he has tried out in the woods. Dewey adocates the use of the scientific method because it demands the interpenetration of thought and action; theories without laboratory work are abstractions, and lab work without theories is meaningless. Though less consistently maintained than in James, Dewey's view of the interpenetration of thought and action should also be taken as including a religious context. God can be defined "scientifically" in Dewey's sense of the term, as he showed in *A Common Faith*.

Perhaps an overly narrow view of pragmatism (i. e., "that is true which makes money;" or "that is true which can be operationally defined;" or "that is true which makes me feel good") can be avoided by retaining our term "mystical pragmatism." The mystic tradition is well known for its insistence that each of us is part and parcel of a wider Self, that God is everywhere and nowhere — in short that all things are inter-related. Terming pragmatism "mystic" situates the interpenetration of thought and action within the widest possible context, to remind ourselves that though objective truth is a myth, nonetheless simple subjectivity is not the answer. James, often accused of advocating simple subjectivity, admonished the readers of *Pragmatism* to pay attention to their previous pragmatic decisions. For, while no preordained law of activity exists, the decisions one makes now or has made in the past will cut off options for the future. Pragmatism, broadly defined, admits that those ideas are true which make a difference, but also subjects competing pragmatic truths to an ever-widening context. Indeed the same advice is given in Royce's principle of "loyalty to loyalty." Be loyal to your cause — that is your function as a human being; but be loyal to that cause which will further the principle of loyalty in the universe. Objectivity has been rejected; subjectivity too has to be rejected — otherwise one winds up in a pollyanna world of self-gratification. Subjectivity can only be rejected by placing pragmatism in a wide context. This is what the term "mystical pragmatism" tries to do, and what seems to arise in the American context.

The Russian context too seems to highlight this broad type of "mystical pragmatism," though it is less well worked out. In a sense, Chaadayev takes the idea of God as a plan of action and attempts to "make it true" in the universe. Herzen developed the philosophy of the act and criticized so-called scientific philosophy as useless unless it could be shown relevant to the problems of individual human beings. Science is overly worshipped by Chernyshevsky — but it is seen as a way of translating thought into action.

The stress on the interpenetration of thought and action differs greatly in the Russian tradition. Because concrete action was impossible for so long, this interpenetration is seen often as only a dream, or is not worked out in detail; it was simply not "pragmatic." In short, the importance of the interpenetration of thought and action is seen in Russia, but much greater difficulty is encountered in holding this importance before the footlights of human consciousness long enough for it to gain a momentum of its own. The result is, unfortunately, often merely a word or a passage on the subject, instead of a well worked out position.

THE IMPORTANCE OF TIME AND HISTORY

With the claim for objectivity rejected and the interpenetration of thought and action avowed, history assumes a vital role. Where Euclidean space was important to a Cartesian outlook, *time* for the Russian and American thinkers symbolizes possibility, the space of operation. It is because time and process are real that the future will not repeat the past in every respect — at least its temporal dimension will be different. To recognize the reality of time is *eo ipso* to recognize the unfinished character of the universe and hence the importance of the human contribution. History stands as the achievements and failures of a person or country over time. As such it too has fundamental importance.

It must be said that the importance of time as real dawned only slowly on these thinkers. History was important for Chaadayev. God specified himself through history; yet Chaadayev wanted to somehow marry this to a view of Divine Providence. So too with Khomyakov: the community was to be seen as important, yet its activity was overshadowed by a view of God as internally complete. Chernyshevsky's scientific materialism leaves little room for the uncertainty of time. Furthermore, the old "scientific" move of operationally defining time in terms of space (i. e., a clock) would certainly underplay its radical dimension. Of the Russians, Herzen came closest to acknowledging the indeterminate quality of history – and this only painfully after the 1848 revolution.

The Americans too were late in recognizing the importance of time for their outlook. For Emerson time seems "at times" to be an illusion, as when he asks why he should go anywhere since he already has everything inside of himself.[206] Nonetheless even Emerson opts for a processive view of the Incarnation with Christ written anew on every face. Royce too affirms the fundamental importance of the Church's role in history. Only in a thoroughly temporal context can a community engage in the interpretation of experience. Yet he too shies away from what this might do by way of redefining God's powers. It is only with James and Dewey that the reality of time is more fully affirmed. James, from the stream of consciousness theory to his world of pure experience, continually viewed both persons and the universe as "never the same, yet never completely different." As he was so fond of saying, "ever not quite" travels along after each philosopher's statement, and there can be no final outlook on the universe until the last person in experience has had his say. Dewey contrasted his view of process with Aristotle's, to show how much more radical the former was. Whereas the acorn became a tree and it was known ahead what the acorn was to become, for Dewey there was no pre-established tree. The universe was not such a tidy spot, and the best one could do was to use the past to prepare for the future.

> . . . change rather than fixity is now a measure of "reality" or energy of being; change is omnipresent . . . [The modern scientist] does not try to define   and delimit something remaining constant *in* change. He tries to describe a constant order *of* change.[207]

Time and history assume fundamental importance in these outlooks because it is through history that "constraining grounds" are placed on the activity of the subject. Objectivity has been renounced, but one cannot go through life from moment to moment, doing whatever one likes whenever one likes. This type of "subjectivity" would be as "timeless" as the objectivity it was meant to replace. Rather is the pragmatist to be seen as dealing with the novelty of the present moment, while at the same time preserving as much of the past as possible. Old truths are important for James; one must remain loyal to as many of them as possible. Dewey talks of the human being as the animal who can preserve his funded experience vicariously – through symbols. In this way the person can come to grips with the confrontation of the present moment by using his funded experience. History then is important as an ever-widening spiral. The pragmatist, then, is no mere subjectivist, but tries to operate in as wide a circle as possible. As James warned: woe to him who ignores his past experience.

COMMUNITY AS CONSTRAINT

When thoughts are hypotheses to be implemented by action, the thinking of one person is easily bound up with the thinking of another, once they both have the same "space of operation." Both the Russian and the American traditions recognized the community as placing constraining grounds upon the subjectivity of the individual.

For Royce an individual is defined in terms of his purpose or will, but that interpretation of experience is essentially communal. I see the world *as* holy *to* you; the process is triadic and ongoing. For Dewey, those works of art are best which can be reinterpreted again and again by a community of observers. Dewey thought the scientific community to be essentially communal, since no one scientist could do everything. Also, all discoveries must be made available to the community of knowers. James too, though weaker in this respect, saw the self as essentially social, and noted that

> No more fiendish punishment could be devised, were such a thing physically possible, than that one should be turned loose in society and remain absolutely unnoticed by all the members thereof.[208]

From the Russian side, Herzen saw the individual as achieving a fuller type of freedom in and through the matrix of human brotherhood. He praised the peasant commune for its decentralized type of context. Khomyakov believed that "truth" was only accessible through a community bound together by love, and opposed individual rationalizations as egocentric abstractions. While Chernyshevsky's ethical outline was one of rational egoism, nonetheless he too praised the peasant commune as a core of socialism for Russia.

The community is important for these outlooks because it is the second type of "constraining ground" placed upon the individual (along with history). What the human being does is important in an unfinished global village, but everyone doing what he wanted would result in mere anarchy. Furthermore there would be no sense of growth, of having gone from something to something else. The American tradition, taking its cue from the procedures of science, refused to set up any one individual as the final arbitrator of the universe. Each individual tried out his hypotheses in an open communal forum. How other people interpret the universe is very important to each person, because other interpretations, *qua* experiments, could affect the status of the forum itself.

For some of the Russians too, "truth" was only accessible through the communal forum; individual systems which purported to leap-frog over the communal context were deemed inadequate and misleading. The community, then, was no mere organization or bureaucracy. Neither subjective or objective, it was the fundamental locus where interpretations of experience were tried out, or made public. Without the community as a life context in and through which each of us comes to be, we would simply fall back into some form of subjectivity or objectivity, in the old sense of these terms. Indeed this seems already to have taken place.

CONCLUSION

The above six themes emerge as fundamental in pre-twentieth century Russian and American thought. To be sure, not all of them exist in each philosopher; indeed many tendencies are visible only from the vantage point of hindsight. Nonetheless taken together they offer one way of operating in the world.

If there is a key point "behind" them it is the affirmation of the vagueness or mystery of the universe. As unfinished, it is fundamentally uncertain, though not merely irrational. As it is immediately presented to the human being, the world is a rich web of concatenations which compel response and commitment. Human actions are important only in a mysterious universe; indeed it is the uncertainty of the situation that compels us to interpret it in one way or another.

But vagueness or mystery is difficult to maintain. First of all it's difficult to be precise about vagueness without losing what you're talking about. As James would say, it's like trying to grab a floating snow crystal to see what it looks like.[209] Secondly, vagueness is often accompanied by the unpleasant feeling of uneasiness. We are always tempted to look for answers, not to highlight the importance of the question. In our contemporary society in America we seem once again to be bewitched with certainty. The sense of "the vagueness of the land" has departed. The problem, however, is even more complex. Not only have we lost this sense of vagueness, but also we are pretending that nothing has been lost at all, or that what has been lost wasn't important to begin with. By a curious form of legerdemain we have turned a "feeling of loss" into a "loss of feeling."

Several popular cultural commentators have caught sight of this issue. Theodore Roszak, for example, believes the present form of objectivity to be technocracy, or "that social form in which an industrial society reaches the peak of its organizational integration."[210] In such a society, the appeal in any argument is to an elite group of technical experts, who rest on the final authority — scientific knowledge. The human person's needs in such a framework are completely technical, and they are defined by experts. An "in here/out there" mentality is adopted.[211] The ideal state of affairs is to have an "in here" (an ego) as empty as possible, so that what is "out there" can be studied objectively. Consequently, a hierarchy is set up between these two; the "in here" is relied upon and trusted, while "out there" is deemed precarious, and in need of control. Finally there takes place what Roszak terms a "mechanistic imperative," an attempt to reduce the person, the "in here," to a well-behaved, self-controlled, electronic nervous system.

It is Roszak's belief that "scientific consciousness depreciates our capacity for wonder by progressively estranging us from the magic of the environment."[212] In his opinion "mystery . . . as the non-human dimension of reality [for tribal man] . . . served to enrich the lives of men by confronting them with a realm of inexhaustible wonder."[213] Whether or not Roszak's identification of technology as the culprit is accurate or merely a red herring, nonetheless his portrayal of cultural malaise rings true. We have lost the sense of mystery or ambiguity in our contemporary culture.

A similar point is made by Philip Slater in his work *The Pursuit of Loneliness: American Culture at the Breaking Point.* Assuming from the outset the critical state of American society, Philip Slater sets himself the task of answering why we are in this time of difficulty. In his opinion, the present American culture frustrates three fundamental desires.[214] First of all, it obliterates the desire for community because of its endless quest for privacy and suburbia. The American has literally boxed himself up in private rooms, private modes of transportation, private gardens, etc. One inevitable result of seeking individual "wrap around" space is that when Americans do bump into one another their interpersonal contacts are often abrasive.

Secondly, contemporary culture denies the basic human need for engagement and involvement, and continually avoids social problems and long-range ramifications of decisions. Americans tend to "solve" problems at the last moment, and then to do so technically, without regard for accompanying dimensions. Our myopia in advocating technological-over-social priority has placed us in a position of alienation where we continually run the risk of being dominated by our machines. Our inability to see contextual relationships has resulted in the creation of ego-reflecting fantasies; the world is only a mirror with which we shadowbox.

Lastly, American society frustrates the desire for dependence and shared resonsibility, and as a matter of fact from childhood on trains the human being to be "creatively independent." This belief in each person pursuing autonomously his own destiny necessitates emotional detachment and by way of backlash, arouses a sense of guilt about our competitiveness and indifference to others.

It seems obvious that the I-Thou relationship offered by a community can only function in a vague or mysterious universe, and that this loss of mystery is the real issue. Slater's phrasing is different, but the problem remains the same. Americans have given up vagueness and replaced it with a kind of antiseptic immediacy. They have adopted the "toilet assumption," the belief that "unwanted matter, unwanted difficulties, unwanted complexities and obstacles will disappear if they are removed from our immediate field of vision."[215] The toilet assumption makes it easier to drop bombs in Viet Nam than to kill a man with a bayonet.[216] By refusing to compare ourselves with anyone else and by dealing solely with ourselves and our fantasies both on an individual and on a national level, we obliterate the possibility of a communal approach to experience. We place our aged into homes and thereby at least tacitly agree with the out-of-sight-out-of-mind doctrine. We accept the Spockian outlook that every individual is unique and foster in our children a sense of competitive myopia. In short, we have become lonely because we have accepted "immediacy" as our cultural imperative. This position is comfortable and secure — change, ambiguity, and vagueness always compel commitment. But there comes a time when the notion of immediacy as a cultural umbilical cord snaps — due to its inherent self-contradictory character. In our opinion we have now arrived at that point.

The two authors discussed above are among the most recognized announcers of our present cultural malaise. They are meant to be merely illustrative — others could certainly have served equally well. Their analyses, though differing in many respects, share two fundamental points. First they agree that what has gone wrong is a general cultural problem — not one that can be characterized within the confines of any one discipline. It is emphatically not the case that the problem exists because one political party is currently in power and that things will be better in four years. Nor is it the case that when the economic crisis is over all will necessarily be rosy. Though each of these issues no doubt contributes to the present cirisis, the above authors seem to hold the opinion that the anomie we suffer is due to a broad cultural situation which is hard to describe, not immediately obvious, and difficult though necessary to change.

Secondly, in their attempts to characterize this cultural problematic, the authors return again and again to one fundamental point – the importance of "vagueness," or "mystery" or "awe" for humankind. This is Roszak's major critique of science; it is also Slater's main argument against the antiseptic world of the immediate present.

What neither author seems to clearly recognize is the complexity of the problem. Not only have we lost this sense of mystery, but we don't want to admit we've lost anything. Or, almost as bad, we admit that this sense of vagueness did exist at one time, but that it was merely one incidental moment in our culture.

The comparisons made between Russia and America in this work are meant to argue against this view. Specifically, they try to show, first, that a sense of the mystery of the land was translated into American philosophy, and that the context *qua* mysterious was deemed extremely important in America, until replaced by an overly "scientific" attitude. Secondly, they argue that the phenomenon was not merely a local quirk. For in Russia too a sense of vagueness was pervasive. To be sure, the similarity was not complete – the political regime in Russia was nothing like that of America. Nonetheless a respect for vagueness and a distrust of abstract reasoning seems to have existed in both countries. While not conclusive in themselves, the comparisons point up the importance of vagueness, and warn against attempts to "describe" or put final boundaries on "mystery." Indeed this seems to be what happened in both countries. Vagueness in America was symbolically ushered out by the Turner thesis, and the move from an agrarian to an industrial economy; a similar and far more disastrous loss of vagueness took place in Russia with the advent of Marxism-Leninism.

One question clearly remains unanswered – *why* did this come about? The comparisons talk only about "the how." The answer clearly goes beyond the scope of this book. But perhaps Gilbert Murray's characterization of a different cultural context is an appropriate beginning. They (and we) suffered a "failure of nerve."[217]

PART II

CONTEMPORARY SOVIET REACTIONS

CHAPTER VII

MARXIST-LENINIST PHILOSOPHY
AND SOCIAL HISTORY

The major thesis of the foregoing has been that a sense of "vagueness" existed in both Russia and America before the turn of the century; furthermore, this sense of vagueness has been lost. An analysis of centomporary Soviet sources shows that not only has this important sense of vagueness been lost, but the loss itself has been repressed. In other words, Marxism-Leninism has turned the "feeling of loss" into a "loss of feeling".

A similar loss has occurred in twentieth century America as one sees from an analysis of contemporary critiques of culture. An unpacking of this repression might be a step in the direction of recovering what has been lost.

The Soviet view on the thinkers discussed above is peculiar to them and conditioned by their Marxist-Leninist belief system.[218] Therefore, it is necessary first of all to discuss Marixst-Leninist ideology, and then dialectical materialism and historical materialism. Finally, the influence of these on Soviet writing of the history of philosophy will be discussed.

THE MARXIST-LENINIST IDEOLOGY

The ideology that supplies the Marxist-Leninist with the principles for judging philosophers and philosophies has the following characteristics:

First of all, philosophy has a very important role to play both in the structure and in the operation of this ideology; the stress on philosophy has been there since the time of Marx and Engels;[219] it was reinforced by Lenin and Stalin;[220] and it seems that the current leaders cannot dismantle this element in the ideology even if they wanted to (for which there is no evidence).[221]

Secondly, instead of being merely speculative, Marxist-Leninist philosophy presents itself as an element in the practical mastery of the world; contrary to Marx, however − who seemed to eliminate theory in favor of practice (or assimilated the former to the latter) − the contemporary Soviets have constructed what amounts to a metaphysical system, which they continue to insist is "practical" in some sense.[222]

Thirdly, contrary to all other contemporary philosophies − which reject human authority as a valid form of argument − contemporary Marxist-

Leninist philosophy still uses the texts of the so-called "classics" of Marxism-Leninism as if they contained some "sacred truth."

Fourthly, Marxist-Leninist philosophy not only declares itself to be "partisan" but also prides itself for this and provides a complex justification for the lack of objectivity; in essence, "party-mindedness" means that one judges everything, especially philosophy, in terms of class-interests.

Fifthly, Soviet Marxist-Leninist philosophy is polemical and aggressive; it uses language like "philosophical front," the "class enemy," "ideological weapons." Although this trait is less noticeable today than it was in 1947,[223] it is continuously and forcefully asserted that the "détente" with the West does not apply to the "ideological front."

Sixth, contemporary Soviet philosophy is dogmatic; the works of the members of this school give evidence of a uniformity that makes the scholastics look pale by comparison. The works of Soviet philosophy still have the flavor of a catechism.[224]

Seventh, there exists among Soviet philosophers, as among the members of any dogmatic school, a special language, flooded with words like "contradiction," "materialism" and "idealism" at every turning.

Finally, since it is the theoretical expression of the class interests of the proletariat, Marxist-Leninist philosophy has to be internationalist; however, as the expression of the ideology of the Communist Party of the Soviet Union, the ideology has taken on some Russian national traits.[225]

DIALECTICAL MATERIALISM

Expositions and explanations of Soviet philosophy in general and of dialectical materialism in particular abound.[226] This presentation of the basic categories and principles of dialectical materialism will limit itself to what is important for an understanding of historical materialism and for making clear why the contemporary Soviet philosophers reject out of hand certain opinions of other philosophers.

Philosophy[227] is defined in Marxism-Leninism as the "science of the most general laws of nature, society and human thought," thus excluding completely such doctrines as existentialism and many forms of neopositivism. The "basic question of all philosophy" serves Marxism-Leninism to determine all other questions of philosophy and world-view. This basic question concerns "the relationship between thought and being, between spirit and nature," and ends up dividing philosophers into two main groups: the idealists who assert the primacy of the ideal over the material; and the materialists who assert the primacy of the material over the ideal.

There are three basic forms of materialism. Mechanicist materialism affirms the primacy of matter but reduces complex phenomena to the mechanical combination of homogeneous material particles. Dialectical materialism affirms the primacy of matter and recognizes as fundamental the dialectical structure of a reality in constant evolution. Vulgar materialism maintains the doctrines of mechanicist materialism − despite the essential corrections made by the materialism of dialectical materialism.

There are three basic forms of idealism, too. Subjective idealists specify that the object of knowledge (the known) is ideal and is located within the knower. Objective idealists specify that the object of knowledge is ideal and is located outside the knower as a reified projection of the knower's consciousness. Masked idealists refuse the distinction between idealism and materialism as fundamental and, above all, refuse to let themselves be classified as one or the other.

Philosophy and the special sciences are related to each other as universal is to particular. The most general laws studied by philosophy are seen in their particular manifestations by the special sciences; hence, an aphilosophic special science is an impossibility. Also, Marxist-Leninist philosophy is not a "science of sciences;" it neither stands above the special sciences, nor does it have an object distinct from theirs.

As for its doctrinal content, Marxist-Leninist philosophy can be reduced to a few simple statements:

First, everything that is, is matter. When asked if thought is matter, Soviet philosphers reply that "it is not matter but is material."[228] All types of idealism and spiritualism are thought to be excluded by this statement. What is not at all clear from the Soviet texts is whether "matter" really means just matter, or means "material things" and the "ground of all things."

Second, all matter is in motion. This is also held to mean that there is no motion without matter, nor matter without motion. Implied in this statement is the further notion that nothing is unchangeable or absolute.

Third, all material motion is dialectical. "Dialectical" can have many meanings. Here, it means "development according to the 'three basic laws of the dialectic.' " These laws are: 1) The unity and conflict of contraries; 2) The transition from quantitative changes to qualitative changes; 3) The negation of negation. The usual exemplifications of these laws are taken from historical materialism. The contraries in the first law are the proletariat and the bourgeoisie: these classes unite to form society but are contrary one to the other. The transition from quantitative changes to qualitative changes comes about when quantitative changes in the way of life of the proletariat (e. g., lowering of buying power, increase in hours of labor, degenerating working conditions, etc.) add up to a demand for revolution, i. e., a qualitative change. Finally, by negating the bourgeoisie, the proletariat negates itself as a class, thus negating the negation.

Fourth, thought is a reflection of being; and social thought is a reflection of social being. This doctrine grounds historical materialism in dialectical materialism.

HISTORICAL MATERIALISM

Historical materialism results from the application of dialectical material-ism to the investigation of society and history, and asks the question as to which is primary, social being or social consciousness. It answers this question by asserting that social being in the form of material production is the basis of the life of society.[229]

Social reality is determined by the dialectical relations between the forces of production (tools, raw materials, etc.) and the relations of production (commercial relations, etc.), where the forces determine the relations. A further dialectic exists between the base of society (the entirety of its economic infrastructure) and its superstructure (social ideas and institutions; ideology, etc.).

History is the history of class conflict and there are five basic stages: primitive society (communal ownership of the means of production); ancient society (e. g., Greece, Rome), also called "slaveholding" society; feudal society (lords and serfs replacing masters and slaves); capitalist society (bourgeois-capitalists and proletarians); and finally, socialism (or "Com-munism" with communal ownership of the means of production, etc.).[230]

Tensions between base and superstructure are reflected in tension between the class of the oppressed and the class of the oppressors and, when aggravated, lead to a "revolutionary situation." Revolution is a period of upheaval in the development of society, in which a transition from one social-historical formation to another is achieved. The deepest cause of a social revolution is the conflict between new forces of production and old relations of production. Revolution is (1) anti-feudal, (2) bourgeois-democrat-ic, and (3) proletarian.

Moribund capitalism (which is dying of its internal contradictions) frantically tries to save itself by resorting to "imperialism" or extension of the class-war to the international scene. As a result, imperialist powers fight among themselves for colonies and markets and with the colonial peoples in order to subject them. The world is divided into two camps, the imperialist camp (of war) and the socialist camp (of peace); between these are the exploited countries of the third world who belong "objectively" to socialism and "subjectively" to imperialism.

In all of this the Communist Party plays a leadership role due to its position as representative of the best interests of the proletariat.

Social consciousness (or ideology) reflects social being. However, social being is always primary. In class society the ideas and institutions of the ideological superstructure serve the interests of the ruling class and are used to oppress the dispossessed. Old social ideas tend to outlive the social being which gave rise to them.[231] The main domains of social consciousness are: political and juridical ideas and institutions, philosophy, art, and religion.[232]

MARXIST-LENINIST HISTORIOGRAPHY OF PHILOSOPHY

For Marxism-Leninism, philosophy forms an essential part of the super-structure. The history of philosophy is, therefore, also part of the super-structure and a tool in the class-war. This historiography of philosophy can be stated for the sake of simplicity in the form of a few basic imperatives.

First, establish the period of the philosophy in question, according to the five main periods of history (as above). Every non-Marxist-Leninist philosophy or philosopher belongs to one of the three main periods — acient, feudal, or capitalist. There are, of course, transition periods; e.g., although the bourgeoisie is reactionary in philosophy, the systems of the early bourgeois periods show traces of being progressive, at least to the extent that they were anti-feudal. Also, there are contemporary systems which constitute anachronisms in their appeal to philosophies of previous periods; e. g., although neopositivism is a completely modern philosophy (running from Hume to Ayer), neo-Thomism has little modern about it and represents a frank return to the out-dated ideas of Aquinas.

Second, distinguish clearly proletarian philosophy from bourgeois philosophy. The former is materialist, scientific, atheistic and progressive; the latter is idealist, superstitious, religious, and reactionary.[233] These two terms (proletarian vs. bourgeois) constitute an adequate and necessary distinction between what is good in contemporary philosophy and what is useless and out-dated.

Third, make certain to establish those who are progressive and those who are reactionary on the contemporary scene. Above all, one has to appreciate the distinction between a philosopher who subjectively belongs to the bourgeoisie but objectively to the proletarian philosophy (e. g., Roy Wood Sellars) and a philosopher who subjectively belongs to proletarian philosophy while objectively he serves the interests of the class-enemy (e. g., Roger Garaudy).

Fourth, determine the deleterious effects of wrong philosophy and highlight the advantages of correct philosophizing. It is incumbent on the Marxist-Leninist historian of philosophy to demonstrate that wrong philosophy has served the interests of religion and reaction in the past and that it now is continuing to serve the interests of counter-revolution. One also should be showing how the correct philosophy arms the proletariat and its party for the fight against the philosophical class-enemy.

Fifth, always argue in function of the truths revealed by the "classics of Marxism" (Marx, Engels, Lenin). There is no better source for a view of history and for the basic principles of any philosophical critique.

Sixth, be "party-minded," i. e., partisan. It is incumbent on every proletarian philosopher to argue from the viewpoint of proletarian philosophical truth. This viewpoint is expressed by the party in its official publications and by party philosophers in their numerous works.

Seventh, serve proletarian internationalism. The class-war has to be carried out on the international scene. All bourgeois are to be attacked and all proletarians must be aided. Here it is important to make all the necessary "subjective-objective" distinctions so that one does not end up attacking a class-ally.

Eighth, be concrete, historical, dialectical, etc. One must observe the unity of theory and practice. There are no "facts" in isolation from one's world-view. Bourgeois "facts" must not be allowed to get in the way of proletarian truth.

PROBLEMS OF SOCIAL AND NATIONAL CONDITIONING

It is clear from all the above that Marxist-Leninist philosophy is a kind of sociology of knowledge (*Wissensoziologie*). The main traits of any philosophy or philosopher are explained primarily in terms of social circumstances. Each philosophical school — and the Soviets are rather peremptory and cavalier in deciding what constitutes one[234] — can be sufficiently and necessarily described by historical period (ancient, feudal, bourgeois), by class status (bourgeois, proletarian), and "objective comportment" (what interests does it actually serve). Every philosopher is described in function of the philosophical school to which he belongs, but also by the historical period and by his class status. The distinction between "objective class status" (or "belongingness") and "subjective class status" is essential to the Marxist-Leninist account of the world. One can belong "subjectively" to the bourgeoisie while belonging "objectively" to the proletariat (e. g., an affluent German who supports Soviet Communist policies).

Although Marxist-Leninist Communism is supposed to be internationalist and opposed to bourgeois nationalism, in actual fact, contemporary Soviet philosphers are – to use Lenin's expression – "great Russian chauvinists" and do use a nationalist criterion in the history of philosophy. For example, Marxism-Leninism views pragmatism as essentially connected with "the American way of life." This un-Marxist "Russification" of Marxism-Leninism is one of the bones of contention between the Soviets and the Chinese Maoists. As a result, there are conflicting criteria at work in the operations of the contemporary Marxist-Leninist historian of philosophy. He is told that he must be "party-minded," but the party changes its mind about which philosophies are serviceable and which are not. He is also told that he should search for the truth but the truth turns out to be the truth of a specific group. He is told that history is essential to an understanding of reality but, in fact, everything is judged in terms of the criteria of today. Finally, the influence of great Russian nationalism is still strong, constituting a social conditioning of sorts but representing an undue intrusion of a non-Marxist element.

CHAPTER VIII

SOVIET REACTION TO
SOME NINETEENTH-CENTURY PHILOSOPHERS

Given the foregoing brief exposition of Marxism-Leninism, we are now in a position to describe both their general outlook on Russian and American philosophy and their specific views on the eight individual philosophers treated in part one. Then, a final chapter will analyze the Soviet position on the six themes described as characteristic of a vague or ambiguous Universe.

THE GENERAL SOVIET VIEW ON RUSSIAN PHILOSOPHY[235]

The history of the Soviet view on Russian philosophy has been the scene of many battles — both valiant and ignoble. No one will forget A. A. Maksimov's attempt to lay the heavy hand of Russian nationalism over the whole of Soviet philosophy, under the aegis of the "fight against bourgeois cosmopolitanism."[236]

Fighting against this temptation to glorify all that is Russian, if only because this country has been the home of the proletarian revolution, is the principle of "proletarian internationalism," according to which — among other things — Russian philosophy is no better than any other pre-Marxist, bourgeois philosophy, and all of the latter were bad.

The work currently being done by Marxist-Leninist historiographers of philosophy falls, fortunately, in between these two schools. We read: "The philosophic thought of the Russian people has traversed a grand and complex historical path."[237] The writing of this history is to serve the needs of the "new Soviet man;" it synthesizes the experiences of the past to contribute to progress in the present and future. Such a history has to be written with a devotion to progress and for purposes of educating the coming generation. Finally, such history serves as a weapon in the class war of the proletariat against the bourgeoisie.[238]

The Soviet account divides the history of Russian philosophy into four periods: the feudal; the transition to capitalism; the development of pre-monopolistic capitalism; and the period of imperialism.[239]

During the feudal period in the history of Russian philosophy, the scene was dominated by religion and mythology. There was a trend toward centralism and the more progressive thinkers were talking in terms of the unity of the people and the land. The "progressive" was he who criticized the Patriarchate and who depended on science. The paradigmatic figure in this regard is Lomonosov.[240]

The period of transition to capitalism was also that of the gradual breakdown of the feudal structures. In reaction to this threat to the old system, Orthodoxy tried to strengthen its position but science and the ideas of the Enlightenment were breaking through. In addition, materialistic views were on the rise "in the form of Deism."[241] The leading figure during this time was Radishchev, a convinced opponent of autocracy and serfdom. Also in existence at this time were the radical views of Pushkin and the Decembrists, as well as the influence of mechanicist materialism and of Schelling.[242] In addition, one has to take account of the progressive views of the Westernizers and the reactionary views of the Slavophiles. It was the revolutionary democrats who were the most progressive pre-Marxists, and the most eminent materialist was Herzen (who qualifies as anti-idealist, anti-metaphysical, historicist, progressist, revolutionist, and who moved toward the dialectic).

The development of pre-monopolistic capitalism was accompanied by the end of serfdom. There was open war between idealism and materialism, best exemplified in the person of Chernyshevsky (whom Lenin called the "great Russian Hegelian and materialist"), for whom man was the central issue.

The economic and social consequences of the reforms of 1861, the development of capitalism in Russia, and the simultaneous strengthening of political reaction led to changes in the distribution of class forces and to intensification of the class war.[243]

However, the philosophic outlook which resulted, *narodnichestvo*, was not any more progressive than the philosophy of Chernyshevsky, not detecting the leading role of the proletariat. It was in the 1880's that the first Marxists (Plekhanov, Zasulich, Aksel'rod) appeared in Russia. It was Plekhanov who popularized the study of the revolutionary democrats. All this progress, however, was met by widespread reaction in the form of positivism and religious idealism (Solov'ev) just before the turn of the century.

The imperialist period saw a radical change in Russian philosophy. With the growth of the proletariat, the development of the class war, the progress of science, the strengthening of the influence of the dialectical-materialist world-view, and dissemination of the ideas of scientific socialism came great changes in the content and nature of the development of philosophy in Russia.[244]

"The Great October Socialist Revolution marked the victory of the dialectical-materialist world-view. The Russian philosophical heritage of materialism became an important element in socialist culture."[245]

A great amount of historical continuity is posited by these Marxist-Leninist premises. The price paid for this is high, however. It consists in suppressing the basic truth that much of pre-Marxist-Leninist Russian philosophy had always been profoundly religious in character and that materialism — whatever it might mean in this context — was a fringe occurrence.[246] In other terms, the price paid consists in ignoring the fundamental importance of mystery or ambiguity for Russian culture.

THE GENERAL SOVIET VIEW ON AMERICAN PHILOSOPHY[247]

In talking about American philosophy, the Soviet historiographer is not as interested in historical accuracy as in getting across a point; namely, that American philosophy is the philosophy of a society in crisis and must, therefore, reflect this crisis in some way.

For the Soviet historian, American thought begins in a religious context but very quickly moves to anti-religion among the revolutionary ideologists. Capitalism arrived with the Revolution in America, along with an anti-Enlightenment fundamentalism. Furthermore, at the end of the nineteenth century, America was seriously influenced by both Darwinism and the conviction that one should get back to basics, i. e., to good old "common sense."

The move into the twentieth century was marked in U.S. thought by empiricism and rationalism. Philosophy was done mainly by people in the academic life and suffered from this stricture. Pragmatism — the specifically American philosophy — is latter-day voluntarism with a strong admixture of biologism. The various "realisms" that have arisen in America are but species of idealism either subjective or objective. From the Soviet point of view, the neo-materialism of Roy Wood Sellars is an interesting attempt which has the virtue of coming close to dialectical materialism. It is refreshing for the Soviets to note the strong influence exercised by the ideas of Marxism on the minds of the progressive intelligentsia of the U.S.

Since American philosophy began and has developed entirely during the capitalist period of history and in a country devoted completely to capitalism, its present state is dependent on the present state of capitalism. According to Jan Bodnar, this state can be described as follows:

There is a world-wide crisis of the capitalist system with its passage to its final stage, imperialism.

Capitalist culture is now mortally wounded and the idealist world-view is in deep crisis.

Furthermore, the working class, armed with the doctrine of scientific socialism and with the revolutionary program for the social reconstruction of society, is entering into the social-political fight.

In other words, the class war is intensifying, while Marxism-Leninism triumphantly spreads across the world uniting progressive forces under the leadership of the Communist Parties.

To combat this, there now exists an intensified effort on the part of the imperialistic bourgeoisie to dominate the world, establish a fascist hegemony, and to liquidate the last remnants of democratic rights and principles.[248]

THE SOVIETS ON CHAADAYEV AND EMERSON

The standard Soviet image of Petr Yakovlevich Chaadayev is that of a man who begins by being very negative on Russia's chances and utopian in his views on society and history. History is a unity of the necessary and the free; Chaadayev stands against both voluntarism and fatalism. He sees individualism as false and even pathological. Man is a combination of the physical and spiritual which Chaadayev sometimes interprets as a parallelism, sometimes as a unity.

The final Soviet word is that Chaadayev comes up with some of the right conclusions but always for the wrong reasons. The following text may serve as a summary statement.

> When Chaadayev speaks about the events which led in the West to ideas of civil rights and freedom, he has in mind not the revolutionary activity of the masses, of classes and of parties against tyranny, oppression and exploitation. Oh, no! Chaadayev was a resolute opponent of revolutionary methods of conflict and refused to see it as contributing to social progress ... The events that are basic, according to Chaadayev, to the individual and social life of man are the spiritual events, the ideas, and the transformations in thought.[249]

Strangely enough, Ralph Waldo Emerson seems to arouse less ire on the part of the Soviets than does Chaadayev. Emerson is described as a spiritualist and a romantic. "Spiritualist" means idealist but in a more fundamental sense than that of Berkeley, etc. For Emerson, everything exists ideally in God;

which brings him close to pantheism. Emerson's personalism consists in his insistence on the individual soul as intermediate between nature and the supernatural. "Romanticism" in the case of Emerson means that, even though he criticized capitalism, he let stand the primacy of the individual.

Although Emerson is appreciated as a pacifist, abolitionist and humanist by Soviet historians of philosophy, it is mainly through his view of nature that they try to "recuperate" him. They act as if his notion of nature were that of science, i. e., empirical, whereas it has a wider and definitely religious dimension. Also, the Soviets choose to stress Emerson's political-social attacks on bourgeois society, without saying that his critique is rooted in his religious views. Finally, these ideas are discussed without taking into account Emerson's "mystical" idea of "regeneration through the land."

THE SOVIETS ON HERZEN AND JAMES

Alexander Herzen is celebrated by the Soviets as a materialist in the best sense, i. e., as a dialectical materialist (actually, "before the fact" since he did not get it via Marx).[250] The Soviets appreciate Herzen's view of history as a process which advances continually, following certain laws and leading to the greater and greater unity of being and thought. His only weakness was that he did not see the pitiless battle between idealism and materialism that permeates the history of all philosophy.

Herzen's main contributions are in the line of social philosophy. It was he that pointed out that the communal village system (*mir*) of land ownership was such as to permit in Russia a transition to socialism without the necessity of going through the capitalist stage. Lenin celebrates Herzen as a fighter against autocracy and for equality.

Although he was profoundly historicist, Herzen remained idealist in his conception of the role of the masses in history and in his maintenance of the state as a necessary political structure. Herzen developed a humanist ethics, based on reason and protecting the rights of individuals. He asserted the rights of life against asceticism.

William James is presented by Soviet philosophers as more dangerous than Emerson but as less dangerous than Dewey. James is accused of being a subjective idealist, a strange accusation since he is also accused of being a neo-realist, and it would seem that the two are irreconcilable. As we have seen, James rejected both "subject" and "object" in the traditional meaning that these terms have had.

James' contribution to the formation of pragmatism is said to be the instrumental understanding of the nature of truth. In other words, the Soviets see James as denying knowledge of essences and as reducing laws of nature to mere heuristic devices (instead of taking them as laws of reality).

The Soviets also accuse James of being a "Machist" which is the traditional Leninist term for a "positivist." What they mean by this is that James was somewhat of a reductionist. This, however, is obviously not true. Just on the surface, it seems impossible to be labeled both a neo-realist and a positivist at the same time. While James did see scientific laws as incomplete in and of themselves, he insisted on the ontological status of the conceptual realm.

The fact that James takes religion seriously is, of course, in no way appreciated by any of the Soviet commentators. The nefariousness of James' involvement with religion appears, according to the Soviets, in his flirting with spiritualism.[251] The neglect of the religious side of James stands as a major omission, since religious themes permeate the entire historical development of his philosophy.

Finally, James is made out to be a typical bourgeois liberal, despite his protests against American militarism.

THE SOVIETS ON KHOMYAKOV AND ROYCE

Alexis Stephanovich Khomyakov usually receives little attention in Soviet writings, although he is appearing more and more as the paradigmatic spokesman of slavophilism.[252]

On the Soviet reading, Khomyakov sees "willing reason" (or God) as the principle of all that exists. The history of the emergence of being is not to be interpreted empirically (as it is by Western historians) but to be seen as the dialectical interplay of freedom and necessity. One must protect the people from Western religion which ruins man and turn to true religion of the "willing reason" as freely creating spirit. Khomyakov was also guilty of a romantic attitude toward Russian feudal socialism, unwittingly supplying people like Danilevsky with nationalist arguments.

Little attention is paid by the Soviets to Josiah Royce because he is, on the one hand, an absolute idealist with his religiosity of the Absolute idea and of Christianity as perduring and, on the other, a social conservative who espouses the reform of capitalism rather than revolution.

One could justifiably ask why the Soviets do not try to recuperate Royce on two accounts: first, his notion of the internal (my will) and external (will of the Absolute) meaning of an idea corresponds to their "absolute and relative truth;" secondly, Royce's notion of a person becoming an absolute individual and the idea that the absolute individual and the single human individual ultimately share the same goal or purpose seems to correlate with the shared goal(s) of the Party and the Party-member.

THE SOVIETS ON CHERNYSHEVSKY AND DEWEY

Nicholas Gravilovich Chernyshevsky is presented by the Soviets as a "Russian socialist utopian, revolutionary democrat, economist, philosopher, sociologist, writer and literary critic."[253] He is an "instinctual socialist" who sees true democracy as possible only under socialism. Feuerbach's anthropologism served Chernyshevsky for the overcoming of German idealism and metaphysics, and for a critique of bourgeois theories of society. Chernyshevsky's only mistake was to remain on what Lenin called the level of "descriptive materialism." Chernyshevsky was a social optimist who thought that the laws of history and society could be known and that something could be done. Although he saw action in view of personal advantage as the motor of history, he also saw the class war that appeared briefly in the events of 1848 as a sign of a new era in social relations.

The Soviets see Chernyshevsky as painfully aware of the paradox of revolution; namely, in order to throw off the yoke of the upper classes, the lower classes have to have leaders who seem automatically to form another upper class — and nothing changes. Therefore, Chernyshevsky ends up as a utopian because he cannot discover the correct, materialist, Marxist solution to this problem — namely, the leadership role of the proletariat and of the proletarian party. He sees the absolute need for revolution but also the absolute impossibility thereof at that time. He turned then to fight for a new morality and against liberalism which he correctly saw to be a bourgeois trick.

For the Soviets, John Dewey emerges as the main enemy in classic American philosophy. This fact illustrates a principle which is basic to all the description and analysis that has been undertaken here — namely, Soviet friendliness toward or enmity to a given philosopher or philosophic system depends in the final analysis not on the basic theoretical stance of the philosopher in question but on the "social harm" that flows either from the theoretical stance, or from his personal activities, or from both.

Dewey qualifies for the title of "enemy number one" through his pragmatism, biologism and instrumentalism. The Soviet philosopher G. A. Kursanov says that pragmatism is subjective idealism, a species of positivism, eclectic (containing elements of vulgar materialism, metaphysics and Kantian apriorism), unscientific, voluntarist, individualist, adventurist and fideist.[254]

Pragmatism itself is of some embarrassment for the Soviets who themselves espouse a sort of "social cash-value" theory. However, they see that Dewey's principle of biological adaptation is contrary to the theory of conditioned reflex, which the Soviets think they get from Pavlov. The Soviets also see that Dewey's instrumentalism — as a self-corrective scientific method — is anti-determinist and, therefore, anti-Marxist-Leninist.

However, all these theoretical positions pale before Dewey's capitulation — like that of all pragmatists — to religion, before his educational theory which ignores social conditioning, and before his rank anti-Communism.

CHAPTER IX

UNDERLYING THEMES IN CONTEMPORARY MARXIST-LENINIST PHILOSOPHY

All the issues pinpointed in Chapter VI as representing touchstones for comparison of Russian and American philosophy in the nineteenth and twentieth centuries are also discussed in Soviet philosophy.

A cursory glance might indicate that these fundamental themes were as central to Marxist-Leninist philosophy as they were to the nineteenth century Russian and American philosophic traditions. Closer analysis, however, indicates that this is not the full story. Though some similarities do exist, differences nonetheless remain; furthermore, some of these differences are fundamental. In particular, the Soviet outlook seems to have lost an awareness of the importance of ambiguity.

ANTI-CARTESIANISM

At first glance, one is tempted to assume that the philosophy of Marxism-Leninism is as anti-Cartesian as are the Russian and American philosophies in the period under consideration. This would be true, first, to the extent that the Soviets consider Descartes to be a dualist who is materialist in his cosmology and idealist in his psychology, whereas the Soviets themselves energetically reject both dualism and idealism, as well as Descartes' mechanicist view of the world.[255] Secondly, there is support for this assumption in the fact that Soviet philosophy rejects the idea of a spectator-ego, looking out at its quantifiable world, as well as any kind of abstractionism. The Soviet view seems to agree with James in making the human being a participator rather than mere spectator; with Royce on viewing man as interpreter; with Dewey's view of experience as a flux in and through which a person comes to be. Finally, they highlight the radical activism of Chernyshevsky and have little trouble with Herzen's philosophy of the act.

However, a philosophy which holds to a reflection theory of knowledge and to psycho-physical parallelism cannot escape the most evident troubles of Cartesianism. By making thought a reflection of being Marxism-Leninism has condemned itself to a futile circle of explanations: is there any continuity of nature between reflecting knower and reflected object? If so, what does a *material* reflection look like? If not, how is the reflecting to be explained? As to the problem of psycho-physical parallelism, there is a long history of inconclusive attempts by Rubinstejn and others to say something consistent on the question.[256] Despite these efforts, Cartesian dualism has not been overcome. It would seem then that the Marxist-Leninists criticize the Cartesian position, but at the same time remain curiously "Cartesian" in outlook.

Most important is the fact that the Soviets *agree* with Descartes in eliminating doubt or mystery from the world. Marxism-Leninism holds the world to be essentially intelligible perforce of certain universal laws inherent in it. Everything in the universe is said to be structured according to the basic laws of the dialectic; which is why dialectically structured minds are able to understand anything in this universe. This sounds very close to the ultimate rationalism that arose from Cartesianism. Mystery and ambiguity are gone.

THE HUMAN BEING AS PARTICIPATOR

The Marxist-Leninist outlook at first glance seems to advocate a deterministic view of history. The latter is divided into five eras, each of which is destined to follow in a prescribed order. From this viewpoint, there would seem to be little or no significance to the individual *qua* participator in the historical process. He would be condemned to stand idly by and to acquiesce in the process, or to try to stop it and be doomed to failure. Either there would be no "space of operation" for the individual human being, or his actions would be clearly subsequent to and dependent upon social and economic forces.

However, this rejection of human being as a participator ignores a basic ambiguity of Marxism-Leninism and the thrust of recent developments in their philosophic outlook. The ambiguity in question is due to the attempt to associate Marx's economic determinism and Lenin's politicial voluntarism in one doctrinal framework. Thus, although all meaning seems to be the work of the Party and seems to be attributed exclusively to the Party, the theory still holds that it is *active* individuals who set things in motion and that it is the vital interests of the "new Soviet man" that are the driving force of the new society.

Whether because of developments in the West or because of internal forces, problems of the person, his desires, intentions, etc., are occupying more and more space in Marxist-Leninist writings, under titles such as "Society and the Person" (*obshchestvo i licnost'*).[257] This is not to say that Communism — which calls itself "socialist humanism" — has become a genuine humanism. It does mean, however, that many of the theses of the Western and Russian philosophers we are treating are not totally foreign to Marxism-Leninism. In a revolutionary theory man has to make some difference and if every man is taking part in the revolutionary transformation of the universe, then every man is in some sense an artist.[258]

For many of the thinkers we have dealt with in Part I, religion was a pre-eminent locus of human participation. It is clear, however, that the twentieth century Marxist-Leninist reaction is resolutely atheist. A little too resolutely, perhaps. Many are the scholars who have pointed out that one of the strongest appeals of the Marxist-Leninist system is that it serves to replace religion.[259] There have also been those who have suggested that many Communist activities replace religious activities.[260] In short, it is not at all clear that the religiosity of an Emerson and a Chaadayev is totally absent from Marxism-Leninism, despite its public opposition to religion. Here too the issue of human choice and participation would seem to be central, though presently hidden from sight.

SCIENTISM VERSUS CONTEXTUALISM

One would think that as revolutionaries and "Leninist voluntarists," the Soviets would have to be advocates of an unfinished and mysterious universe. For, if the universe is not open in some sense, then there is little for a revolutionary to do.

However, the open universe has been rejected by Marxism-Leninism. It would seem that this is due mainly to the fact that such an unfinished and mysterious universe presents a threat. It requires a free and honest encounter of the creative subject with his or her environment and eliminates the need for and utility of a party with all the answers. Marxism-Leninism presents "proletarian partisan-ship (party-mindedness)" as constituting "true objectivism" — i. e., that which makes it possible to see the real course of history.

These restrictions on contextualism are reinforced by the rigid dogmatism of Soviet "scientism." The historical origins of this scientism are easy to find. Marx and Engels were fascinated by science — by Darwin and by all the discoveries being made and applied in their lifetimes.[261] They pretended to bring socialism "from utopia to science." Marx thought he made political economy into a science, by detecting the "four iron laws of history" which were to bring capitalism down with historical inevitability.[262] Lenin, too, did his main intellectual work in a period of intense scientific development. His *Materialism and Empirio-Criticism* fights through a whole series of problems of interpretation of science, and of the use of science in political quarrels.

This is why early Soviet philosophy was quickly caught up into the whirl of science and why questions of philosophy of science (in their meaning of the term) have continued to figure prominently in Soviet journals.[263] What is meant by "science" here is a typically nineteenth century notion. The universe is a well-ordered whole, without any external factor needed to explain it or its order. Knowledge of it has progressed to the point where we know all the essential contours. What needs to be done is to fill in the details within these contours. This is a collective enterprise, a task of the scientific community which serves the best interests of mankind and can do so better under the guidance of the enlightened (i. e., the Party). This scientific knowledge is not abstract and speculative. It feeds a technology which is gradually freeing man and mankind from superstition, fear, etc.

Therefore, modern man's Promethean task is already laid out for him in the form of the scientific challenge. However, the universe that is attacked by science is not ambiguous and certainly is not unfinished. To use a scholastic distinction, *quoad se* (in itself) the universe is perfect, closed and complete, *quoad nos* (as far as we can tell) there is still a lot in the universe to be known and done.

In short, for Marxism-Leninism, science is an important tool, the utility of which lies precisely in the elimination of the mystical and the vague.

THEORY AND PRACTICE

It should be obvious — if only from the Marxist-Leninists' violent and unceasing protests — that pragmatism and "theory and practice" have little in common. According to the Soviet account, American pragmatism is tainted with biologism and/or with religiosity. This in itself is enough to distinguish it from "theory and practice."

For the Soviets, thought and action interpenetrate in the sense that without theory there is no practice and without practice there is no theory.

In other words, every element of thought originates in some form of activity; every item of thought is ultimately confirmed in activity.

In contrast to American pragmatism which involves reference to "personal satisfaction," the "dialectical unity of theory and practice" is a radical requirement of the real relations between social human beings and the world. In other words, we as dialectically structured beings know (dialectically) a dialectically structured reality; theory and practice therefore are united by the very fact that all who do theory do practice and all who do practice do theory. There is nothing done which is not done dialectically. The difference between a correct and a wrong dialectical unity of theory and practice is that the former involves correct knowing of and conforming to the dialectical nature of reality.

Whereas many forms of pragmatism either stress individual effort or at the very least acknowledge its importance, Soviet emphasis on *partijnost'* tends in the other direction. Although it is true that the Party knows truth and does good (necessarily), it is also true that the individual member is encouraged to "assent" to the Party-line and to "work" for the new society. Thus, there is a sense in which the human being is a participator and there is even a sense in which the universe is incomplete or unfinished. This unfinished dimension, however, remains clearly subordinate in Soviet, as opposed to nineteenth-century American, thought. The incompleteness is not ontological; it is epistemological and intimately bound up with the problem of relative and absolute, on the one hand, and time and history, on the other.

TEMPORALITY AND HISTORICISM

Since — for the Marxist-Leninist — both the material universe and the social world are in evolution, both are at least temporally incomplete. Far from this incompleteness being an essential trait of the universe, it is rather one that will be inevitably overcome. Furthermore, since any individual's knowledge of this incompleteness is unfinished, it too has to be completed and this happens in the Party. The importance of the Party as objective referent comes out in the Soviet account of truth. True knowledge is both relative and absolute, and subjective and objective. True knowledge is, for the Soviets, relative because what is known is not only just a portion of what exists but also what exists is constantly in the course of developing. True knowledge, however, is also absolute because what is there to be known is there as an intelligible whole; the true is the whole and the whole is the true. True knowledge is subjective because it always exists in and through an individual knower who can have only his own limited view of the world. It is objective because the content of true knowledge represents the world as it is. It is clear that the bearer of true knowledge as relative and subjective is the individual person. It is also clear that true knowledge as absolute and objective is the possession of the Communist Party which is "the honor, conscience," etc., of the proletariat which, in turn, represents the best interests of mankind (of all epochs). Therefore, the finishing and completing of the unfinished and incomplete is the work of the individual only in and through the Party. This conception of history as rational and determinate seems far from what people like James and Herzen had in mind.

In short, the Soviets — like the ancient Hebrews — are dealing with two different and seemingly irreconcilable notions of time: the temporality of the relative and subjective and the historicity of the absolute — in short, human time and cosmic time. The great difficulty in understanding what the Soviets are about is often due to the confusion of these two notions.

What counts, then, is not the development of the individual and/or the time-perception of the person, but the time-line of the Party and the Party's perception of the historical flow. They often talk as if the Party's perception *is* the historical flow.

COMMUNITY

It is true that both Marxism-Leninism and several of the nineteenth century figures studied in Part I place great emphasis on the importance of community. In spite of this, the notion of community seems to be much more narrowly defined by the Soviets.

Community for Marxism-Leninism has to be seen in the context of the class-war which has formed the content of history up to now. Capitalist communities serve exploiters' interests and represent rank subjectivism in relation to the individuals in them. Such subjectivism supports idealism, religion, reaction, etc. Truly human organizations can be formed only when class-war has been eliminated, and classes along with it. Only the establishment of Communism makes it possible for men to associate freely, to the benefit of all.

In the American tradition the notion of community remained important throughout. Royce's notion of a community of interpreters has been discussed in Part I. Dewey's notion of God as the name given to the "ideal project" or goal of the community was developed in *A Common Faith*. During the latter part of his life James developed a quasi-mystical notion of community in terms of "the compounding of consciousness."[264] The most striking difference lies of course in the role of the religious element — admitted by all the American authors and also evident in several of the Russian thinkers we have mentioned.

It could be that, whatever the differences between them, the ideas of "God" and of "authentic humanity" share at least this fact: both can function as the lynchpin of social-ethical systems. Dare one go so far as to say that whoever rejects theism falls necessarily into a humanism which appears as the mirror-image of the theistic world? Or that the distinction between theism and humanism is non-existent, "pragmatically" speaking?

FINAL THOUGHTS

How important is the cultural context for the development of any philosophical position or school? Although the foregoing analysis does not claim to be conclusive, it has tried to show that contexts cannot be ignored.

We have suggested that there existed similarities between Russia and the United States toward the turn of the century which provide a valuable aid in understanding the interplay between a philosopher and a cultural context. In so doing, we admit of course that similarities and/or differences are never complete. Again, our purpose has been to assert that some similarities exist, and that they are worth noting.

What, then, have we shown?

That in two large — continental and populous — countries which have come to play dominant roles (culturally, politically, militarily, etc.) on the contemporary scene a basic cultural shift took place at approximately the same historical era.

We have described this cultural shift as a "closing of the experiential context" as a medium in and through which growth takes place. The key aspect of this closing turns out to be a loss of mystery as symbolic of opportunity. On the psychological level this might be termed a loss of nerve. Most of the philosophers compared in Part I tried in some way to preserve a sense of mystery. In other words, they reacted against the loss of context *qua* mysterious.[265] Among the changes which resulted from the loss of an indeterminate context, we have highlighted the following aspects:

First, there is revocation of the healthy revolt against Cartesianism, and reinstitution of both dualism and scientism.

Second, there is growing departure from considering humans as active co-creators, and an abandonment of everything to mechanical determinism.

Third, there is a resolute rejection of openness and unfinishedness in any regard, with a (one is tempted to say "irrational") return to "autonomous rationality."

Fourth, as a direct consequence of the reassertion of autonomous rationality, there is loss of a sense of the correlation of theory and practice — of what we called "mystical pragmatism." The problems of subject and object reappear along with all the confusions they engender.

Fifth, "mechanical time" and "objective history" are re-established and the change-fixity dialectic becomes unclear.

Sixth, community is removed as the *locus* of individuals, with anarchy as consequence.

Seventh, the issue of the importance of ambiguity has polarized itself into one of religion vs. science. Because indeterminacy is seen as a threat, the conviction exists that the farther one gets away from the "religious" and the closer to the "scientific," the better off one will be.

Eighth, in the United States mystery has been lost but some culture critics have recognized this and pointed out the need to regain this sense of ambiguity or awe. In the Soviet Union mystery has also been lost but this is not admitted. This "feeling of loss" has been turned into "the loss of feeling" and this is strictly maintained.

Aristotle said that philosophy begins in wonder, and this statement seems no less true now than it was 2500 years ago. The human being is perhaps best defined as a "questioning animal." The interesting thing about a person is that he or she can ask questions at all — not the specific answers given to them. If this is so, to lose the ability to question is to cease to exist as a human being. There are no questions in *Brave New World.*

However, questions have a precondition: they only arise in an indeterminate or unfinished or mysterious context. Questions are only real (as opposed to rhetorical) when actual choice is involved. ("Will you be here at midnight?") Only in an indeterminate universe are questions taken at their full value.

The nineteenth-century American and Russian contexts were radically uncertain or mysterious. Furthermore, they "realized" in some way that this indeterminacy was essential. Although some specific questions could be answered, nonetheless the cultural context should always be seen as fundamentally mysterious. It is ironic that only in an uncertain or mysterious world can one function as human being. In this case, however, the irony rings true. Perhaps William James said more than even he realized when, at the close of the nineteenth century, he asked for "the re-instatement of the vague to its proper place in our mental life." [266]

NOTES

1   Marshall McLuhan, *Understanding Media: The Extension of Man* (New York: McGraw-Hill, 1965), *passim*.

2   Daniel J. Boorstin, *The Americans: The National Experience* (New York: Vintage, 1965), p. 219.

3   Ralph Waldo Emerson, "Nature", in *Selected Writings of Ralph Waldo Emerson* edited by William H. Gilman (New York: Signet, 1965), p. 197.

4   Daniel J. Boorstin, *The Americans: The Colonial Experience* (New York: Vintage, 1958), p. 5.

5   *Ibid.*, p. 7.

6   *Ibid.*, p. 96.

7   William James, *Pragmatism* (New York: Longmans, Green, 1908), p. 197ff.

8   This view of the frontier is perhaps most adequately mirrored in John Dewey's description of the scientific method. See John Dewey, *Reconstruction in Philosophy* (Boston: Beacon, 1957), Chapters 2, 3, *passim*. It should also be noted that only the more positive aspects of the frontier experience have been highlighted here. This should not be taken as implying that no negative aspects existed.

9   Emerson, "The American Scholar", *op. cit.*, p. 230.

10   John Dewey, *The Quest for Certainty* (New York: Capricorn, 1960), p. 306.

11   The image of man as a sculptor is a pervasive one in the writings of William James. See especially *The Principles of Psychology*, 2 vols. (New York: Dover, 1950), Vol. 1, pp. 288–9; *Pragmatism*, p. 246ff.

12   Frederick Jackson Turner, *Frontier and Section: Selected Essays of Frederick Jackson Turner* (Englewood Cliffs: Prentice Hall, 1961), pp. 38, 61.

13   *Ibid.*, p. 61.

14   *Ibid.*, p. 62. For an excellent analysis of the frontier spirit in American culture, see John J. McDermott, "The American Angle of Vision", *Cross Currents*, 1965, pp. 69–93, 433–60.

15   Henry Nash Smith, *Virgin Land: The American West as Symbol and Myth* (New York: Vintage, 1950), p. 297.

16   McDermott, *op. cit.*, p. 454.

17   Smith, *op. cit.*, p. 303.

18   McDermott, *op. cit.*, pp. 436–7. For an outstanding portrayal of the present crisis, see Robert C. Pollock, "Dream and Nightmare: The Future as Revolution", in *American Philosophy and the Future*, edited by Michael Novak (New York: Charles Scribner's Sons, 1968), pp. 60–86.

19   Philip Slater, *The Pursuit of Loneliness: American Culture at the Breaking Point* (Boston: Beacon, 1970), Chapter 1, *passim*.

20   Theodore Roszak, *The Making of a Counter Culture* (New York: Anchor Press, Doubleday, 1969), p. 252.

21   Joseph L. Wieczynski, "The Frontier in Early Russian History", *The Russian Review*, April 1972, Vol. 31, # 2, pp. 110–6, p. 110. For a more personal comparison of the United States and Russia, see Yuri Glazov, "The Passing of a Year . . .", in *Studies in Soviet Thought* Vol. 15 (1975), 4, pp. 273–290.

[22] V. V. Zenkovsky, *A History of Russian Philosophy*, 2 vols. (New York: Columbia University Press, 1953), Vol. 1, p. 28.

[23] Nicholas Berdyaev, *The Russian Idea* (Boston: Beacon, 1962), p. 2.

[24] James H. Billington, *The Icon and the Axe*: *An Interpretative History of Russian Culture* (New York: Vintage, 1970), p. 6.

[25] For further elucidation of this point see the works of Ivan Kireyevsky and Alexis Khomyakov, in *Russian Philosophy*, 3 vols., edited by James Edie, James Scanlan, and Mary-Barbara Zeldin (Chicago: Quadrangle, 1965), Vol. 1, pp. 155–269.

[26] Zenkovsky, *op. cit.*, Vol. 1, p. 5.

[27] *Ibid.*, pp. 30–31; Billington, *op. cit.*, pp. 59–60.

[28] Billington, *op. cit.*, p. 7.

[29] *Russian Philosophy*, *op. cit.*, Vol. 1, pp. 161–2.

[30] For the following see, for example, R. D. Charques, *A Short History of Russia* (New York: Dutton, 1956), Cahpters 2, 3, 4, *passim*.

[31] Berdyaev, *op. cit.*, p. 12.

[32] Charques, *op. cit.*, p. 101.

[33] Zenkovsky, *op. cit.*, Vol. 1, p. 6.

[34] James, *The Principles of Psychology*, Vol. 1, p. 254.

[35] Zenkovsky, *op. cit.*, Vol. 1, p. 150.

[36] *Ibid.*, p. 151.

[37] Raymond T. McNally (transl. and commentary), *The Major Works of Peter Chaadayev* (South Bend, Indiana, 1969), p. 30.

[38] *Ibid.*, p. 32.

[39] *Ibid.*, pp. 37–38

[40] *Ibid.*, p. 205.

[41] *Ibid.*, p. 207.

[42] *Ibid.*, pp. 215–6.

[43] *Ibid.*, p. 25.

[44] *Ibid.*, p. 157.

[45] *Ibid.*, p. 91.

[46] *Ibid.*, p. 41.

[47] *Ibid.*, Introduction, p. 13.

[48] *Ibid.*, p. 118.

[49] *Ibid.*, p. 116.

[50] *Ibid.*, p. 196.

[51] *Ibid.*, p. 142–143.

[52] *Selected Writings of Ralph Waldo Emerson* edited by William H. Gilman (New York: Signet, 1965), p. 52.

[53] *Ibid.*, p. 101.

[54] *Ibid.*, p. 107.

[55] *Ibid.*, p. 221.

[56] *Ibid.*, p. 186.

[57] *Ibid.*, p. 73.

[58] *Ibid.*, p. 172.

[59] *Ibid.*, p. 238.

[60] *Ibid.*, p. 240.

[61] *Ibid.*, p. 263.

[62] *Ibid.*, p. 281.

[63] *Ibid.* p. 218

[64] *Ibid.*, p. 197.

[65] *Ibid.*, pp. 201–2.

[66]   *Ibid.*, p. 222.

[67]   *Ibid.*, p. 217.

[68]   *Cf. ibid.*, p. 226.

[69]   *Ibid.*, p. 189.

[70]   *Ibid.*, p. 70.

[71]   *Ibid.*, p. 230.

[72]   *Ibid.*, p. 192.

[73]   *Ibid.*, p. 91.

[74]   *Ibid.*, p. 242.

[75]   Loren Baritz, *City on a Hill: A History of Ideas and Myths in America* (New York: John Wiley and Sons, Inc., 1964), p. 268.

[76]   Nicholas Lossky, *History of Russian Philosophy* (New York: International Universities Press, 1951), p. 56.

[77]   For the following, see Zenkovsky, *A History of Russian Philosophy*, Vol. 1, p. 290.

[78]   Alexander Herzen, *Selected Philosophical Works* (Moscow: Foreign Languages Publishing House, 1956), p. 575.

[79]   *Ibid.*

[80]   Alexander Herzen, *From the Other Shore, and The Russian People and Socialism* (introduction by I. Berlin), (New York: World Publishing Company, 1963), p. 38.

[81]   *Ibid.*, p. 127.

[82]   *Ibid.*, p. 6.

[83]   Alexander Herzen, *The Memoirs of Alexander Herzen*, Parts I and II (translated by J. D. Duff), (New York: Russell and Russell, 1967), p. 245.

[84]   Herzen, *Selected Philosophical Works*, p. 109.

[85]   *Ibid.*, p. 111.

[86]   *Ibid.*, p. 516. See also p. 85 where Herzen says: "Guided by the letter of science alone, they have stifled every vestige of feeling, of warm sympathy. Deliberately and with great effort they have hoisted themselves to the level of indifference to all things human and firmly believe that they have attained the loftiest of heights."

[87]   Herzen, *From the Other Shore, and The Russian People and Socialism*, p. 98.

[88]   Herzen, *The Memoirs of Alexander Herzen*, p. 36.

[89]   Herzen, *Selected Philosophical Works*, p. 31.

[90]   *Ibid.*, p. 98.

[91]   Herzen, *From the Other Shore, and The Russian People and Socialism*, p. 98.

[92]   Herzen, *Selected Philosophical Works*, p. 21.

[93]   *Ibid.*, p. 74.

[94]   *Ibid.*, p. 79.

[95]   *Ibid.*, p. 106.

[96]   Herzen, *From the Other Shore, and The Russian People and Socialism*, p. 140.

[97]   *Ibid.*, p. 180.

[98]   *Ibid.*, p. 190.

[99]   *Ibid.*, p. 129.

[100] See, for example, *ibid.*, pp. 134–5.

[101] William James, *The Writings of William James*, ed. with an introduction by John J. McDermott (New York: Modern Library, 1968), p. 7.

[102] *Ibid.*, pp. 7–8

[103] *Ibid.*, p. 723.

[104] For the following, see *ibid.*, pp. 21–74.

[105] *Ibid.*, p. 70.

[106] *Ibid.*, p. 29.

[107] *Ibid.*, p. 34.

[108]   *Ibid.*, p. 45.
[109]   *Ibid.*, p. 47.
[110]   James, *The Principles of Psychology*, Vol. 1, pp. 244–5.
[111]   *Ibid.* p. 245
[112]   James, *The Writings of William James*, p. 45.
[113]   James, *Pragmatism*, pp. 46–7.
[114]   *Ibid.*, p. 53.
[115]   *Ibid.*, pp. 49–50.
[116]   *Ibid.*, p. 201.
[117]   *Ibid.*, p. 252ff.
[118]   *Ibid.*, pp. 168–9.
[119]   See, for example, Peirce's "How to Make Our Ideas Clear" and "The Essentials of Pragmatism", in *Philosophical Writings of Peirce*, edited by Justus Buchler (New York: Dover 1955), pp. 23–41, 251–68.
[120]   See, for example, Dewey's "Context and Thought" and "An Empirical Survey of Empiricisms", in *On Experience, Nature and Freedom*, edited by Richard Bernstein (New York: Bobbs-Merrill, 1960), pp. 88–110, 70–87.
[121]   See, for example, A. N. Whitehead, *Modes of Thought* (New York: Capricorn Books, 1958), Part Three: "Nature and Life", pp. 173–232.
[122]   James, *Pragmatism*, p. 61.
[123]   *Ibid.*, p. 61.
[124]   *Ibid.*, p. 241.
[125]   The two texts are respectively *Pragmatism*, p. 256ff; p. 205. The reference is to a personal discussion, but a similar statement by the same person can be found in *The Writings of William James*, Introduction, p. xxiiiff.
[126]   See in this regard, William James, *A Pluralistic Universe* (New York: Longmans, Green, 1909), pp. 181–221; and *The Varieties of Religious Experience* (New York: Longmans, Green, 1914), pp. 508–19.
[127]   James, *The Writings of William James*, p. 735. The original source of the quote is Fitz-James Stephen, *Liberty, Equality, Fraternity*, (Second Edition; London, 1874), p. 353.
[128]   See above, Chapter 1.
[129]   Josiah Royce, *The Problem of Christianity*, 2 vols. (Chicago: Henry Regnery Company, 1968), Vol. 2, p. 64.
[130]   *Ibid.*, p. 37.
[131]   *Ibid.*, p. 51.
[132]   John E. Smith, *The Spirit of American Philosophy* (New York: Oxford Universtiy Press, 1966), p. 91.
[133]   Royce, *op. cit.*, pp. 64–65.
[134]   *Ibid.*, p. 111.
[135]   *Ibid.*, p. 42.
[136]   *Ibid.*, p. 150.
[137]   *Ibid.*, p. 312.
[138]   Cf. Josiah Royce, *The Philosophy of Loyalty* (New York: Macmillan, 1924), p. 138.
[139]   Royce, *The Problem of Christianity*, Vol. 2, p. 387.
[140]   *Ibid.*, p. 424.
[141]   *Ibid.*, p. 102.
[142]   *Ibid.*, p. 90. (italics added)
[143]   See, e. g., *The Problem of Christianity*, Vol. 2, pp. 373–4: "The world is the process of the spirit. An endless time-sequence of events is controlled, according to this account, by motives which, endless in their whole course, interpret the past to the future."

[144] *L'Eglise Latine et le Protestantisme au point de vue de l'Eglise d'Orient*: *Receuil d'articles sur des questions religieuses écrits à différents époques, et à diverses occasions* par A. S. Khomiakoff (Lausanne et Vevey: B. Benda, Libraire – Editeur, 1872), p. 398. [Hereafter referred to as "*EL*."]

[145] *Ibid.*, p. 64.

[146] Cf. Khomyakov, "On Humboldt", in *Russian Intellectual History, An Anthology*, edited by Marc Raff (New York: Harcourt, Brace, and World, 1966), p. 211.

[147] Cf. Zenkovsky, *A History of Russian Philosophy*, Vol. 1, p. 187.

[148] Khomyakov, *EL.*, p. 12.

[149] Khomyakov, as quoted in Nicholas Riasanovsky, "Khomyakov on Sobornost," *Continuity and Change in Russian and Soviet Thought,* edited by Ernest J. Simmons (New York: Russell and Russell, 1967), p. 184.

[150] Cf. V. V. Zenkovsky, *Russian Thinkers and Europe* (Ann Arbor: American Council of Learned Societies, 1953), p. 54.

[151] Zenkovsky, *A History of Russian Philosophy*, Vol. 1, p. 192.

[152] Khomyakov, *The Church Is One* (New York: Eastern Orthodox Catholic Church in America, Division of Publications, 1953), p. 23.

[153] Cf. Zenkovsky, *Russian Thinkers and Europe*, p. 54.

[154] See, for example, the famous text from Khomyakov's last unfinished work, found in *Russian Philosophy*, Vol. 1, p. 251ff: "I gave the name *faith* to that faculty of reason which apprehends actual (real) data and makes them available for analysis and awareness by the understanding [*Verstand*]. Only in this area do the data still have the fullness of their character and the marks of their origin. In this area, which precedes logical consciousness and which is filled with a living consciousness that does not need demonstrations and arguments, man realizes what belongs to his intellectual world and what to the external world. Here, by the touchstone of his free will [*volia*], man perceives what in his (objective) world is produced by his creative (subjective) activity and what is independent of it . . .

"But, on the other hand, we can think about the object of consciousness only within the laws or categories of consciousness itself."

Here Khomyakov, on the one hand, seems to want to get beneath conceptual dichotomies, to penetrate beneath the phenomenal world to the "all;" on the other hand, he reintroduces the subject/object dichotomy and with it all the one-sidedness he seems to want to avoid.

[155] Khomyakov, *EL.*, p. 301.

[156] Cf. above, p. 69.

[157] Zenkovsky, *Russian Thinkers and Europe*, pp. 55–6.

[158] An excellent analysis of this issue is to be found in Patrick O'Leary's "The Trinitarian Ecclesiology of Alexis Stephanovich Khomyakov" (unpublished dissertation presented to the Faculty of Theology, University of Fribourg, Switzerland, 1970). "If a writer neglects the historical dimension of the Incarnation, it is very likely that he will also neglect the historical and human dimension of the Church. This is certainly true of Khomyakov. His theology of the visible and invisible Church contains very profound insights, but it does have the defect of separating the visible Church from the society of men who belong to the Church." (p. 80.)

[159] Khomyakov, *EL.*, pp. 259–60.

[160] *Ibid.*, p. 260.

[161] In other words, Khomyakov identified Christianity too closely with the Russian people – he became too nationalistic. Geographically speaking, he limited the process of the Incarnation to one country. Here again he selected the internal over the external.

[162] See above, Chapters 1–4.

[163] John Dewey, *Art as Experience* (New York: Capricorn, 1934), p. 13. [Hereafter referred to as *AE*.]

[164] *Ibid.*, p. 14.

[165] *Ibid.*, p. 19.

[166] *Ibid.*, p. 56.

[167] *Ibid.*, p. 214. See also p. 162.

[168] *Ibid.*, p. 341.

[169] In the sense that Gabriel Marcel uses the term. See, for example, *Being and Having* (New York: Harper Torchbooks, 1965), pp. 123–124.

[170] Dewey, *AE*, p. 343.

[171] Dewey, *Reconstruction in Philosophy*, pp. xxix–xxx.

[172] *Ibid.*, Chapter 3, *passim*.

[173] John Dewey, *Experience and Nature* (New York: Dover, 1958), p. 358.

[174] Dewey, *AE*, p. 84.

[175] Charles Edward Gauss, "Some Reflections on John Dewey's Aesthetics", in *Journal of Aesthetics and Art Criticism*, Vol. 19, 160–1, pp. 127–32; p. 131.

[176] Dewey, *AE*, p. 194. The whole other aspect of the question, i. e., whether art/science is related to politics or ought to be, is a rich topic in itself. However, it goes beyond the scope of this paper.

[177] Dewey, *Experience and Nature*, pp. 364–5.

[178] N. G. Chernyshevsky, *Selected Philosophical Essays* (Moscow: Foreign Languages Publishing House, 1953), p. 282.

[179] *Russian Philosophy*, Vol. II, p. 12.

[180] Chernyshevsky, *Selected Philosophical Essays*, p. 286.

[181] *Ibid.*, p. 287

[182] *Ibid.*, p. 292.

[183] *Ibid.*, p. 365.

[184] *Ibid.*, p. 366.

[185] *Ibid.*, p. 340.

[186] *Ibid.*, p. 343. See also p. 489.

[187] *Ibid.*, p. 70.

[188] *Ibid.*, p. 371.

[189] *Ibid.*, p. 362.

[190] *Ibid.*, p. 440.

[191] *Ibid.*, p. 445. See also pp. 374, 508.

[192] *Ibid.*, pp. 374–5. (italics added)

[193] *Ibid.*, p. 124.

[194] *Ibid.*, p. 128.

[195] *Ibid.*, p. 125. At another place, however, he says that the "qualities of any group of people are the sum total of the qualities of the individuals comprising that group" (p. 220).

[196] *Ibid.*, p. 92.

[197] *Ibid.*, p. 128.

[198] *Ibid.*, p. 492.

[199] *Ibid.*, p. 433.

[200] *Ibid.*, p. 435.

[201] *Ibid.*, p. 435.

[202] *Ibid.*, p. 379.

[203] William F. Woehrlin, *Chernyshevskii, The Man and the Journalist* (Cambridge: Harvard University Press, 1971), p. 337.

[204] E. Lampert, *Sons Against Fathers* (Oxford: Clarendon Press, 1965), p. 213.

[205] William James, *The Will to Believe and Other Essays in Popular Philosophy* (New York: Longmans, Green, 1927), p. ix. James is here quoting B. P. Blood, *The Flaw in Supremacy* (New York, 1893).

[206] See, for example, *Selected Writings of Ralph Waldo Emerson*, pp. 275–6: "The soul is no traveller; the wise man stays at home . . . Travelling is a fool's paradise. Our first journeys discover to us the indifference of places."

[207] Dewey, *Reconstruction in Philosophy*, p. 61.

[208] James, *The Principles of Psychology*, Vol. I, p. 293.

[209] James, *ibid.*, Vol. I, p. 244.

[210] Roszak, *The Making of a Counter Culture*, p. 5.

[211] For the following, see *ibid.*, p. 217ff.

[212] *Ibid.*, p. 252.

[213] *Ibid.*, p. 262.

[214] For the following, see Slater, *The Pursuit of Loneliness: American Culture at the Breaking Point*, p. 5ff.

[215] *Ibid.*, p. 15.

[216] For the following, see *ibid.*, p. 22ff.; p. 5ff; p. 62ff.

[217] Gilbert Murray, *Stoic, Christian and Humanist* (Freeport: Books For Libraries Press, 1969), p. 64.

[218] For the Soviet analysis of contemporary U. S. thought, see A. S. Bogomolov, *Anglo-amerikanskaja burzhuaznaja filosofija epochi imperializma* (Anglo-American Bourgeois Philosophy of the Era of Imperialism) (Moscow: Mysl', 1964. 420str.); and, by the same author, *Burzhuaznaja filosofija SShA XX veka* (Bourgeois Philosophy in the U.S.A. in the Twentieth Century) (Moscow: Mysl', 1964. 342str.); N. S. Juliana, *Burzhuaznye ideologicheskie techenija v SSgA* (Bourgeois Ideological Currents in the U.S.A.) (Moscow: Nauka, 1971. 135str.); *Sovremennaja burzhuaznaja ideologija v SSgA* (Contemporary Bourgeois Ideology in the U.S.A.) (ed. Ju. A. Zamoshkin, etc. Moscow: Mysl', 1967. 342str.); Jan Bodnar, *O sovremennoj filosofii SShA* (On Contemporary U.S. Philosophy) (Moscow: Socekgiz, 1956. 246str.); I. Lingart, *Amerikanskij pragmatizm* (American Pragmatism) (Moscow: IIL, 1954. 254str.); G. A. Kursanov, *Gnoseologija sovremennogo pragmatizma* (The Epistemology of Contemporary Pragmatism) (Moscow: Socekgiz, 1958. 193str.); as well as the relevant sections in *Istorija filosofii* (History of Philosophy) (= *IF*) (Moscow: Nauka, 1957–65. 6 vols.) and in *Filosofskaja enciklopedija* (Philosophic Encyclopedia) (= *FE*) (Moscow: Sov. Encik., 1962–72. 5 vols.)

[219] Despite his abandonment of philosophy for political economy, Marx never stopped "philosophizing." Engels was a continual neophyte in philosophy. He heard lectures by Schelling and learned most of the rest of the philosophy he knew from Marx.

[220] Lenin's political activities did not keep him from writing purely philosopical works. Stalin was definitely not a philosopher but under his patronage Marxist-Leninist philosophy prospered.

[221] On the importance of philosophy for Soviet ideology and of the latter in the operation of the Party, see J. M. Bochenski, "Ideology, Power-Politics and Dialectics," in *Studies in Soviet Thought*, Vol. 3 (1963), pp. 53–5.

[222] Proof: "theory" and "practice" are "dialectically related categories" in Marxism-Leninism; that is, they are elements in a metaphysical system. For Marx, on the contrary, the overcoming of philosophy in practical activity involves the transcendent recuperation of the former in and by the latter.

[223] In the "good old days," words like "cesspool" and "garbage" occurred with dizzying frequency.

[224] One of the most striking evidences of this is the italicizing of passages in Soviet books on philosophy.

[225] Cf. *Istorija filosofii v SSSR* (= *IFS*) (The History of Philosophy in the USSR) (Moscow: Nauka, 1968. 3 vols.), Vol. I, p. 10.

[226] Cf. J. M. Bochenski, *Diamat* (Dordrecht: Reidel, 1963)and G. A. Wetter, *Dialectical Materialism* (London: Routledge, 1958).

[227] A standard presentation of dialectical materialism is to be found in *Osnovy marksistskoj filosofii* (Fundamentals of Marxist Philosophy) (Moscow: Gospolitizdat, 1958) and in the article on the same in *FE I*.

[228] Cf. V. N. Kolbanovskij, 'Pravil'no li utverzhdat,' chto soznanie material'no? ' (Is it Correct to Assert that Consciousness is Material?) in *Voprosy filosofii* (Questions of Philosophy) 1954, *4*, pp. 236–8.

[229] Cf. *IFS I*, p. 10.

[230] During Krushchev's reign, intermediate periods were introduced between capitalism and final socialism (e. g., accelerated construction of socialism, etc.); fortunately, these have, for the most part disappeared, with him.

[231] The "lag principle" is operative in many facets of Soviet philosophy. It is almost as important as the dialectic for explaining why what happens does happen.

[232] The triad of philosophy, art and religion has its origins, it seems, in Hegel. It has caused all sorts of problems for "scientific atheism." For, whereas all proponents of neo-Communism agree that the new society has to have new politics, new law, new philosophy and new art, any temptation to call for a new religion was effectively squelched by Lenin.

[233] Cf. *IFS I*, p. 11.

[234] For example, "objective idealism" is a sack big enough to include both Thomas Aquinas and Bertrand Russell.

[235] For further details, see *IFS, IF* and *FE*.

[236] See the first issue of *Voprosy filosofii* (= 1947, *1*) for the beginning of this fight.

[237] *FE 4*, p. 533.

[238] Cf. *IFS 1*, pp. 7–21.

[239] Cf. *FE 4*, pp. 533–41.

[240] The basic principle in this kind of recuperation is "the enemies of my enemies are my friends."

[241] *FE 4*, p. 534.

[242] Schelling exerted a strong influence both on Russian philosophy and on Marx through Engels.

[243] *FE 4.*, p. 538.

[244] *Ibid.*, p. 539.

[245] *Loc. cit.*

[246] Using the principle, mentioned in note 240, "materialist" covers anyone in history who did something nice.

[247] Cf. *FE1*, pp. 48–52 and the works cited in note 218, above.

[248] Bodnar, *op. cit.*, p. 9.

[249] M. M. Grigor'jan, 'Chaadaev i ego filosofskaja sistema' (Chaadayev and His Philosophic System) in *Iz istorii filosofii* (From the History of Philosophy) (Moscow: AON, 1958), p. 138.

[250] An older theology made a distinction between "vincible" and "invincible" ignorance. The same type of distinction exists – for the Marxist-Leninists – between mechanicist materialism which pre-existed Marxism, and "vulgar" materialism which has exactly the same content as mechanicist materialism but is "vincible" because it could benefit from Marxism which already exists.

[251] Cf. *FE 1*, p. 471.

[252] Cf. *FE 5*, pp. 443–4.

[253] *FE 5*, p. 479.
[254] Kursanov, *op. cit.*, pp. 193–4.
[255] Cf. *FE I*, pp. 447–50.
[256] All these problems are discussed in T. R. Payne, *S. L. Rubinstejn and the Philosophical Foundations of Soviet Psychology* (Dordrecht: Reidel, 1968).
[257] Ten volumes under this title have been published in Leningrad under the editorship of B. G. Anan'ev; but, the main development has been in Eastern Europe, e. g., Adam Schaff, the "Praxis" group, etc.
[258] See, in this respect, Dewey, *AE*, pp. 337–43.
[259] Wetter, *op. cit.*
[260] In East Germany, there is a crass attempt to substitute civil ceremonies for religious ones.
[261] Engels' *Dialectic of Nature* is a monument to this as is his talk at the graveside of Marx.
[262] These four laws are: (1) the falling profit-rate; (2) increasing monopolisation; (3) pauperization of the proletariat; (4) cyclical crises.
[263] Cf. *Bibliographie der sowjetischen Philosophie*, Volumes V and VII, especially the indices.
[264] For Royce's notion of community, see *The Problem of Christianity*, 2 vols (Chicago: Henry Regnery, Gateway Edition, 1968), Vol. II, pp. 107–276, as well as above, pp. 44–48. For Dewey's notion of "God," as the communal ideal, see *A Common Faith* (New Haven: Yale, 1934), *passim*, but especially p. 42ff; for James' views on the "compounding of consciousness," see *A Pluralistic Universe* (New York: Longmans, Green, 1909); pp. 131–221.
[265] It must be admitted, however, that this is less true of some of them than of others. This is particularly so as "science" becomes important (i. e., in Dewey and Chernyshevsky).
[266] James, *The Writings of William James*, p. 45, and above, p. 38.

INDEX OF
NAMES AND TITLES

Italic numbers relate to the Notes on pp. 103–11

SOVIETICA

Publications and Monographs of the Institute of East-European Studies
at the University of Fribourg/Switzerland
and the Center for East Europe, Russia and Asia
at Boston College and the Seminar for Politicial Theory and Philosophy
at the University of Munich

1. BOCHEŃSKI, J. M. and BLAKELEY, TH. J. (eds.): *Bibliographie der sowjetischen Philosophie*. I: *Die 'Voprosy filosofii' 1947–1956*. 1959, VIII + 75 pp.
2. BOCHEŃSKI, J. M. and BLAKELEY, TH. J. (eds.): *Bibliographie der sowjetischen Philosophie*. II: *Bücher 1947–1956; Bücher und Aufsätze 1957–1958; Namenverzeichnis 1947–1958*. 1959, VIII + 109 pp.
3. BOCHEŃSKI, J. M.: *Die dogmatischen Grundlagen der sowjetischen Philosophie (Stand 1958). Zusammenfassung der 'Osnovy Marksistskoj Filosofii' mit Register*. 1959, XII + 84 pp.
4. LOBKOWICZ, NICOLAS (ed.): *Das Widerspruchsprinzip in der neueren sowjetischen Philosophie*. 1960, VI + 89 pp.
5. MÜLLER-MARKUS, SIEGFRIED: *Einstein und die Sowjetphilosophie. Krisis einer Lehre*. I: *Die Grundlagen. Die spezielle Relativitätstheorie*. 1960. (Out of print.)
6. BLAKELEY, TH. J.: *Soviet Scholasticism*. 1961, XIII + 176 pp.
7. BOCHEŃSKI, J. M. and BLAKELEY, TH. J. (eds.): *Studies in Soviet Thought*, I. 1961, IX + 141 pp.
8. LOBKOWICZ, NICHOLAS: *Marxismus-Leninismus in der ČSR. Die tschechoslowakische Philosophie seit 1945*. 1962, XVI + 268 pp.
9. BOCHEŃSKI, J. M. and BLAKELEY, TH. J. (eds.): *Bibliographie der sowjetischen Philosophie*. III: *Bücher und Aufsätze 1959–1960*. 1962, X + 73 pp.
10. BOCHEŃSKI, J. M. and BLAKELEY, TH. J. (eds.): *Bibliographie der sowjetischen Philosophie*. IV: *Ergänzungen 1947–1960*. 1963, XII + 158 pp.
11. FLEISCHER, HELMUT: *Kleines Textbuch der kommunistischen Ideologie. Auszüge aus dem Lehrbuch 'Osnovy marksizma-leninizma', mit Register*. 1963, XIII + 116 pp.
12. JORDAN, ZBIGNIEW, A.: *Philosophy and Ideology. The Development of Philosophy and Marxism-Leninism in Poland since the Second World War*. 1963, XII + 600 pp.
13. VRTAČIČ, LUDVIK: *Einführung in den jugoslawischen Marxismus-Leninismus Organisation. Bibliographie*. 1963, X + 208 pp.
14. BOCHEŃSKI, J. M.: *The Dogmatic Principles of Soviet Philosophy (as of 1958). Synopsis of the 'Osnovy Marksistkoj Filosofii' with complete index*. 1963, XII + 78 pp.
15. BIRKUJOV, B. V.: *Two Soviet Studies on Frege*. Translated from the Russian and edited by Ignacio Angelelli. 1964, XXII + 101 pp.
16. BLAKELEY, TH. J.: *Soviet Theory of Knowledge*. 1964, VII + 203 pp.
17. BOCHEŃSKI, J. M. and BLAKELEY, TH. J. (eds.): *Bibliographie der sowjetischen Philosophie*. V: *Register 1947–1960*. 1964, VI + 143 pp.
18. BLAKELEY, THOMAS J.: *Soviet Philosophy. A General Introduction to Contemporary Soviet Thought*. 1964, VI + 81 pp.

19. BALLESTREM, KAREL G.: *Russian Philosophical Terminology* (in Russian, English, German, and French). 1964, VIII + 116 pp.
20. FLEISCHER, HELMUT: *Short Handbook of Communist Ideology. Synopsis of the 'Osnovy marksizma-leninizma' with complete index.* 1965, XIII + 97 pp.
21. PLANTY-BONJOUR, G.: *Les catégories du matérialisme dialectique. L'ontologie soviétique contemporaine.* 1965, VI + 206 pp.
22. MÜLLER-MARKUS, SIEGFRIED: *Einstein und die Sowjetphilosophie. Krisis einer Lehre.* II: *Die allgemeine Relativitätstheorie.* 1966, X + 509 pp.
23. LASZLO, ERVIN: *The Communist Ideology in Hungary. Handbook for Basic Research.* 1966, VIII + 351 pp.
24. PLANTY-BONJOUR, G.: *The Categories of Dialectical Materialism. Contemporary Soviet Ontology.* 1967, VI + 182 pp.
25. LASZLO, ERVIN: *Philosophy in the Soviet Union. A Survey of the Mid-Sixties.* 1967, VIII + 208 pp.
26. RAPP, FRIEDRICH: *Gesetz und Determination in der Sowjetphilosophie. Zur Gesetzeskonzeption des dialektischen Materialismus unter besonderer Berücksichtigung der Diskussion über dynamische und statische Gesetzmässigkeit in der zeitgenössischen Sowjetphilosophie.* 1968, XI + 474 pp.
27. BALLESTREM, KARL G.: *Die sowjetische Erkenntnismetaphysik und ihr Verhältnis zu Hegel.* 1968, IX + 189 pp.
28. BOCHEŃSKI, J. M. and BLAKELEY, TH. J. (eds.): *Bibliographie der sowjetischen Philosophie.* VI: *Bücher und Aufsätze 1961–1963.* 1968, XI + 195 pp.
29. BOCHEŃSKI, J. M. and BLAKELEY, TH. J. (eds.): *Bibliographie der sowjetischen Philosophie.* VII: *Bücher und Aufsätze 1964–1966. Register.* 1968, X + 311 pp.
30. PAYNE, T. R.: *S. L. Rubinštejn and the Philosophical Foundations of Soviet Psychology.* 1968, X + 184 pp.
31. KIRSCHENMANN, PETER PAUL: *Information and Reflection. On Some Problems of Cybernetics and How Contemporary Dialectical Materialism Copes with Them.* 1970, XV + 225 pp.
32. O'ROURKE, JAMES J.: *The Problem of Freedom in Marxist Thought.* 1974, XII + 231 pp.
33. SARLEMIJN, ANDRIES: *Hegel's Dialectic.* 1975, XIII + 189 pp.
34. DAHM, HELMUT: *Vladimir Solovyev and Max Scheler: Attempt at a Comparative Interpretation A Contribution to the History of Phenomenology.* 1975, XI + 324 pp.
35. BOESELAGER, WOLFHARD F.: *The Soviet Critique of Neopositivism. The History and Structure of the Critique of Logical Positivism and Related Doctrines by Soviet Philosophers in the Years 1947–1967.* 1965, VII + 157 pp.
36. DEGEORGE, RICHARD T. and SCANLAN, JAMES P. (eds.): *Marxism and Religion in Eastern Europe. Papers Presented at the Banff International Slavic Conference, September 4–7, 1974.* 1975, approx. 195 pp.